S0-BFA-696

Doghouse to *Dollhouse* for **Dollars**™

Using Design Psychology to Increase Real Estate Profits

Jeanette Fisher

ΦΤΠ **Family Trust Publishing**
Lake Elsinore, California, Las Vegas, Nevada

Doghouse to Dollhouse for Dollars™
Using Design Psychology to Increase Real Estate Profits

© 2005 Jeanette Fisher. All rights reserved.

Family Trust Publishing
(951) 678-3369
Printed in the United States of America
http://www.Family-Trust.us
http://DoghousetoDollhouseforDollars.com
Orders: 800-246-5161

No part of this book may be reproduced by any means in any form, photocopied, recorded, electronic or otherwise without written permission from the publisher except for brief quotations in a review.

ISBN 0-9749328-0-9

Includes glossary and index

Edited by Enicia Fisher
Photographs by Jeanette Fisher, unless otherwise credited

Disclaimer: This publication is designed to provide accurate and authoritative information in regard to the subject matter covered. It is produced with the understanding that the authors are not engaged in rendering legal advice or other professional service. If legal advice or other professional assistance is required, the services of a competent professional should be sought.
    —*from a declaration of principles adopted by a Committee of Publishers and Associations*

Rights of Use Statement

No individual or corporation may use the content of this book or Jeanette Fisher's *Doghouse to Dollar$ Workbook*, ideas from her other books, websites, or articles to advise, teach, or train others for profit.

If you're using the book to teach a college-level or professional course, you have permission to photocopy no more than 10 pages for handouts to your students (you must include copyright information on all photocopies). Beyond that amount you need to contact the publisher for permission or consider assigning the book as a textbook.

If you wish to teach private courses or seminars, it would not be legally appropriate to present *Doghouse to Dollhouse* content or solicit students based on the concepts in this book. The trademark *Doghouse to Dollhouse for Dollar$* is a registered service mark and cannot be used by anyone who is not contracted and licensed by Family Trust Publishing, LLC. The only courses entitled to represent *Doghouse to Dollhouse for Dollar$* are administrated by individuals personally trained and contracted by Jeanette Fisher. The only people qualified to conduct inservice training sessions in the use of her methods are members of her personal staff. For further information, contact: Ted Blake, Publisher, 18475 Grand Ave. Lake Elsinore, California <tedblake@family-trust.us> http://Family-Trust.us

About the Author

 Jeanette Fisher helps home owners create homes for glorious living and top-dollar sales. She also works with her husband fixing and flipping houses in Southern California.

Jeanette discovered the psychology of residential design the hard way in 1986. She and her family restored an 1878 Queen Anne Victorian home, which later became the Minute Maid Orange Juice Bed & Breakfast. While undertaking this 6,000 square foot rehabilitation, Jeanette discovered that interior design details significantly influence residents' happiness.

She researched how design details influence emotions at the University of Florida Architectural Library and obtained further materials on the psychological impact of design from the Harvard University Department of Architecture. With over 15 years of research experience in Design Psychology, Jeanette teaches college courses on Design Psychology and real estate investing.

Books by Jeanette Fisher
Published by Family Trust Publishing

Sell Your Home for Top Dollar—FAST!
   Design Psychology for Redesign and Home
   Staging
Staging Homes for Top-Dollar Sales
   A Workbook for Applying Design and Marketing
   Psychology Strategies
Doghouse to Dollar$ Workbook
   Turn "Yucks into Bucks" Investor's Guide
Credit Help!
   Get the Credit You Need to Buy Real Estate
Introduction to Design Psychology
   Designing for Emotional Well-being and Productivity
   (University Textbook)
Coming soon:
Joy to the Home Series: Design Psychology for
Happiness and Well-Being
Saving Sara: Love Heals
Credit Repair Workbook and Letters
Color Psychology for Glorious Living
   (University Textbook)

Dedication

With love to my husband Brian, my "shift-F7," who cooks so I can write, and to our amazing family.

Introduction

Forget what you know about fixing up houses to make money. The rules of bland, white-painted walls and boring beige carpeting changed. After discovering how our emotions are influenced by our homes (Design Psychology), we found that using design details based on psychology to fix-up distressed properties greatly increased our profits.

Forget about talking people out of their homes and other so-called "no-money down" schemes. We have a realistic plan that works for you to find a bargain property and obtain reasonable financing from banks, with little or no money down. We also perfected a method using psychology to market transformed property for maximum profit.

This book begins your journey into the real estate business with important information about credit and financing. Following these basics gives you a firm foundation to become a successful investor. The later chapters on using Design Psychology to transform doghouses into dollhouses are the heart of the book.

Abbreviated Contents

Chapter One

Discovering the Possibilities

More millionaires have earned their money in real estate than in any other type of business. Our family makes far more money in real estate than in any other career. We will show you how we do this and share our money-making secrets. Through our family enterprise, we have transformed over thirty properties, generated great income, and secured profitable investment property for our future.

Most investors who write books about their methods brag about their successes but rarely mention their failures. Though we've had more successes than failures, our family has also lost money on real estate, and we will share these stories as well.

As Oscar Wilde said, "Experience is the name everyone gives to their mistakes." Adopt our successful methods, avoid our costly mistakes, and join the real estate multi-millionaire investor's circle.

Apply our methods and turn doghouses into dollhouses for dollars. Reach financial independence with a little knowledge, inspiration and work. Follow our step-by-step guidelines from credit help to finding, financing, fixing, and selling your property for maximum profit. Learn how the psychology of residential design increases your potential real estate profits.

Baby Steps towards the Ultimate Dream

My husband Brian and I didn't start out as real estate investors. We simply wanted a home for our family. We stretched our limited income and bought our first property in Huntington Beach, California. I could barely wait to try out on my first home what I had learned in college interior design classes. Brian and I worked hard on our first home and didn't fix this house to make money—we fixed it up out of love. However, when we sold the property a few years later, we profited greatly because the housing market had significantly appreciated. *Lesson Learned: we could basically live for free in a house that we owned because we got all our expenses, and much more, back after the sale.*

Our next home for our growing family took us to the San Bernardino Mountains in Crestline, California. This five-bedroom house needed more work than the previous property. We continued learning about home improvement and interior design. Since we had learned about the value of real estate from our first home's profits, we kept this property when we bought our next home. We rented the mountain home for extra income and secured future potential earnings from appreciation.

The House that Sold Itself

We purchased our first investment property, a really dirty doghouse, in Apple Valley, California. We worked on this fixer-upper as a family weekend project, and we learned much more about repairs and renovation in the process. Brian learned how to create a family room out of a garage. He and our twelve-year-old son Evan installed sliding glass doors and a wood-burning stove. They almost lost the structure and learned the hard way about shoring up—supporting with a beam—when cutting into walls. Brian also learned not to install wall-to-wall carpeting. The savings do not equal the effort involved.

We painted the entire home inside and out, adventuring into our now common practice of mixing paint from "oops" paint. We created a new color, "Mohave Sand," by mixing rejected tan, brown, and yellow paints. Recently, we drove by this home and saw that the paint is still there after *twenty-five* years!

Just when we had finished our hard work, our baby daughter Sara became seriously ill. We didn't even list the house for sale because we spent our days and nights in the hospital beside our daughter. But something about the way we fixed up the house attracted a buyer who called me in the hospital to make an offer. To this day, I still do not know how those buyers found me. We really needed extra income and this sale reinforced to us that we could easily make money in real estate. *Lesson learned: turning a dirty doghouse into a dollhouse pays well for part-time work.*

Mistakes in Purchasing Real Estate

Because we became over-confident in our real estate savviness, we next moved back to Newport Beach, California. We paid too much for a house with high interest and a balloon payment second (a large payment due prior to the mortgage being paid off). Not only was the house too expensive, but the real estate market in California had changed. The house wasn't worth what we had paid for it and we were unable to refinance the second. You can learn from our mistakes: secure a decent interest rate, and avoid balloon payment seconds. Also, stay abreast of real estate trends in your local market.

We had to start all over at rock bottom. Since we were able to do this successfully, you too can learn how to build a real estate dynasty from nothing.

Victorian Dream Home Renovation

Some time later, we moved our family to Palatka, Florida for our daughter's benefit. (Sara had survived her serious illness but developed severe disabilities and ongoing medical problems.) The services for children with disabilities were better at that time in Florida than in California. My interest in interior design spurred the desire for the ultimate fantasy home—a three-story Queen Anne Victorian.

My Victorian dream, a dilapidated 6000-square-foot circa 1878 home, taught us how to restore almost any property. This project involved much more than simple painting or remodeling. We rebuilt porches and railings, replaced the gigantic support beam under the front of the house, added on a breakfast room and a spa room, and created bathrooms out of extra spaces. Brian and Evan blew up a jack while shoring up the side of the home, climbed up huge extension ladders and cut into the house, and started a fire using paint stripper.

Our ten-year-old daughter Katie fell through the kitchen floor soon after we moved in, so we tackled the kitchen first. Like many old houses, our kitchen was added on and not built with the craftsmanship quality of the rest of the house. Our entire family worked together to totally rebuild the ramshackle kitchen. We pulled down cardboard walls and discovered newspaper insulation covering frayed electrical extension cords used as wiring. Brian and Evan ripped up rotted sub-flooring and found decaying support beams. Tearing down the ratty ceiling was almost as difficult as rehanging it. Instead of replacing all the fifties style cabinets, we used an antique icebox and Hoosier cabinet for storage. We left enough room for a commercial glass door refrigerator, big enough to hold groceries for our large family. Finally, we painted, wallpapered, and added accessories.

However, after all our hard work and my ill-conceived design plan, the kitchen *felt* all wrong! This is when I undertook the task of researching the psychology of interior design. I spent years researching how our surroundings affect our feelings. Our home became a testing ground for my ideas. We spent ten years doing rooms over and over again and learning more than just the usual tricks of the trade. I learned how to make fabulous stencils and redesigned the kitchen, which finally *felt* right.

During this time, Evan studied architecture at the University of Florida and then at Harvard. I went with Evan to the University to do my research and he helped me from Boston. I broke down all of the elements of interior design and researched how these details influence our physiological and psychological responses. Understanding how decorating details affect emotions is fully covered in my book *Joy to the Home: Design Psychology for Happiness and Well-Being.*

Within ten years, we had transformed the dilapidated haunted house into a gorgeous show-quality home. The neighborhood also changed during this time: before we moved in and renovated, every single house was painted white.

After we painted our Lady seven brilliant colors, many neighbors joined in the exciting adventure of painted Ladies.

Azalea House Bed and Breakfast, Palatka, Florida

Because we could no longer carry Sara upstairs, we sold our beloved Victorian dream home and its next owners established a Bed & Breakfast in the home. Soon after, Minute Maid featured our Lady on its orange juice containers in a Bed & Breakfast giveaway.

Southern Belle Transformation on the River

We moved from the grand Victorian to a nearby 1920's home on the St. Johns River. Vacant and neglected, this southern belle "Tara" property awaited our restorative touch. Using techniques we developed in our prior old-house experience, we cranked out a total restoration and put our house on a historic home tour in a few months.

Because Sara was in and out of the hospital often during this time, we employed Design Psychology to create a serene and joyful home. We cleared a wide swath of jungle to enlarge our peaceful river view. To keep the landscaping tranquil, we only planted white flowering plants near the house and kept the large lawn expanse uncluttered.

Some special touches enhancing joyful feelings included: adding happy colored glass inserts into the interior French doors and painting the entry a pale rosy pink (which looks creamy to the untrained eye). Elise designed an uplifting swag stencil for Sara's bedroom and used amber crystals that captured the sunlight.

Unfortunately, Sara could no longer handle Florida's humidity, so we moved back to California where she could breathe easily in the desert climate. Our friend Ruth moved from California to Florida to enjoy the serenity we created and we received a substantial paycheck when she bought our house.

Shacks Makeover to Bell Pond Cottages

We found two lakefront distressed shacks in Lake Elsinore, California. A large sign on the property advertised the land's potential. These "substandard houses" needed extensive work as well as a large sum of upfront cash. Because banks would not finance the property, we asked for and received short-term owner financing. We repaired the houses, painted, added decks with gingerbread, landscaped, and dug a huge Koi pond—bell shaped, hence the name Bell Pond Cottages. Using Design Psychology, we created an alluring tropical paradise. Then we refinanced the property and got all of our money back, plus a large paycheck for our work.

Bell Pond wasn't even for sale when a Realtor called me with an offer we couldn't refuse. We nearly doubled our purchase price in only ten months! *Lesson learned: using Design Psychology pays higher returns.*

Barn Converted to Guesthouse

We moved down the lake to a larger home and bought the barn next door for $30,000, which we converted into a guesthouse. After the remodeling, we financed the guesthouse and recovered more than our costs, including purchase. Four years later, this property appraised for $285,000 and we refinanced it to buy more investment property.

Evan and Natalie's Lakeview Dollhouse

Our son and his wife bought their first home from the VA—Veterans Administration—for $94,000. This VA repo was a dirty doghouse with a great view. Besides a total clean up and paint inside, my son and daughter-in-law did minor renovations and landscaping.

Evan and Natalie chose not to replace the carpeting or do any major alterations. Evan switched out heavy wood shelves with glass shelves in the living room, added a beautiful wood mantelpiece, and installed custom built-in bookcases in the family room. They upgraded simple light fixtures and plumbing fixtures to dress up the dated look. Natalie did major cleaning with the help of her mother and painted with help from our family. After a month of work and three months of enjoyment, Evan decided to work full time in Newport Beach.

The property sold in *four days* to the second party to see the house. At the sales inspection, it was determined that the property needed a new roof to close escrow, so they used $2,000 of the sales proceeds to repair the leaky roof. It did not cost them any out-of-pocket expenses. With a total investment under $10,000, Evan and Natalie sold their dollhouse for $137,500. Our family loves part-time work that pays about twenty thousand dollars for a couple of month's work!

Evan and Natalie followed his dream of moving back to his childhood home and bought a fixer near Newport Beach. They totally refurbished an out-of-date property and created a fabulous home for their family.

HUD Repo Transformed into Orange Tree Cottage

We continuously search for good real estate finds, especially opportunities to buy repossessed homes. The Federal Housing Administration (FHA), part of the Department of Housing and Urban Development (HUD), insures the bank's mortgage loans and pays the bank in a foreclosure, thereby taking title to foreclosed property.

Three years ago, we took advantage of this program and purchased a HUD repossession for $48,000. (This is the house pictured on the cover.) Within a month, we transformed this doghouse, originally a two bedroom dirty mess, into a three bedroom dollhouse. We painted everything inside and out, added sprinklers, sod, window boxes with flowers, lace curtains, new lighting fixtures, and had a new roof installed. Brian divided a back patio-room into a dining room and a third bedroom. For appraisers to count a room as a bedroom, it needs a closet, so we bought a closet-type armoire at Wal-Mart and attached it to the wall.

After spending around $5,000 to remodel and transform the property, we listed the home and it sold in three hours for more than the asking price! We earned about $68,000 for one month of labor!

To teach our children about making money, we set up a point system on this project. Every worker received one point for each fifteen minutes of work. At the end of the project, we divided the profits according to the points earned. Now our teenagers won't even consider working for minimum wage!

Repo Remodeled into Sugar Plum Cabin

Never rely on HUD's list to be accurate: we found a four bedroom, two-story home listed as two bedrooms. This 2000-square-foot mountain cabin had been on the list for a long time during snow season. We bid way under the listed minimum bid and won the purchase for only $110,000.

When we closed on the cabin and got the electricity on, we saw that the toilet was falling through the floor. Take a flashlight with you to view vacant doghouses! The electricity is never on at a HUD repo and almost never on in a vacant house.

Abandoned in the front yard, the bathtub overflowed with dirt and debris. We used "Restore4" to clean the bathtub and did not need to pay for it to be refinished. We painted the outside of the bathtub with the same paint used on the exterior of the cabin. Bringing exterior colors inside makes the entire home feel harmonious. Your buyer may not notice the psychology of color you apply, but they will *feel* it.

Although Sugar Plum Cabin is a little farther away than we usually would drive for an investment project, this has been the most fun experience. We spent more money on gas and had to buy extra furniture so we could stay over night while we worked on the project. We soon found ourselves spending more time at "work" than at "home" and realized the cabin had become our special retreat!

We love Sugar Plum Cabin so much, we added a no-cost second mortgage, and got our investment money back along with sufficient funds to "float it," or pay for it, for a year. Because we received more cash out from our second loan than our total cash invested, in the end, we got a fantastic and fun second home for free!

Daughter Katie at Sugar Plum Cabin

The four-bedroom a few doors down recently sold for $339,000. We expect to sell our adorable

Sugar Plum Fairy's home for more, whenever we decide to give up our romantic retreat.

Elise and Dan's First House

Our daughter Elise and her husband Dan, married for one year and still in college, decided to buy their first investment property before buying their first home. They used their first time homebuyer's option to buy a house with no money down from HUD. Their winning bid of $104,700 reinforced our stand—you do not need to bid twenty thousand dollars over. This was not years ago; don't let real estate agents bully you into bidding too much on a HUD repo. You need to buy right to make a good profit.

This dreadfully dirty doghouse turned out to be more work than we bargained for. Twenty-three foot high ceilings required nightmare tall scaffolding. We painted the entire interior and hired professional painters to paint the exterior fascia. We saved money by buying "oops paint" and great light fixtures from ReStore (Habitat for Humanity's thrift store).

Brian installed a new tile countertop in the kitchen. Elise made a wall water fountain and a bathroom countertop out of glass mosaics. Dan and Brian put in sprinklers and sod in the front yard. They planted a couple of trees, a few bushes, and pretty flowering perennials.

We had carpet roll ends installed. This carpeting normally sells for $38 per yard. By having one roll end installed up the stairs and two other roll ends installed in the bedrooms, we saved an enormous amount of money. We finally finished the dollhouse and were happy with the $40,000 paycheck. *Lesson learned: No more super tall rooms needing painting without a professional painter!*

Fifties Fixer Becomes Valley View Ranch

We bought this fixer from an owner-agent for $110,000 with a quick escrow and immediate occupancy for my mother and sister. After two years and our restoration work, the property more than doubled in value. We recently refinanced it to get cash out. I like getting paychecks for our work without selling the property. We kept this property as a rental so we could revisit this property again in a couple of years for more equity.

This home has everything most people want— three bedrooms, two bathrooms, two-car garage, terrific fireplace, striking view, wine cellar, and a large yard. But it also has a terrible floor plan, which actually works well for our current tenants. To get to the main bedroom, you need to walk through another bedroom. To get to the third bedroom, you need to walk though the laundry room.

Because of this strange layout, we got creative in showing the property. We showed the home to the appraiser by going through the kitchen into the laundry room, out the side door, around to the back yard, and then back in to the bedroom. We painted the laundry room and made it as pretty as a formal entry to help with the awkward floor plan. *Lesson learned: using psychology to stage and show property increases market value.*

20-year-old Dawn's Real Estate Profits

At the young age of twenty, our family friend Dawn bought her first HUD house. She fixed it up, sold it herself, and made enough money to buy her second fixer house with all cash.

Dawn sold her second house for $44,000 more than her purchase price before she finished fixing it. Dawn then paid cash for her third repossessed house and when she sold that one, she had enough money to buy herself a custom truck with a custom paint finish, and still pay cash for another house.

Dawn bought houses that needed only cosmetic work, not heavy construction. Dawn did all of the painting inside and out. She put in all new light fixtures and all new plumbing fixtures in the homes. She had new carpeting installed and readied the homes for move-in condition. *Dawn did all this—three doghouses—in nine months!*

Next, Dawn bought another home for $125,000 and flipped it for $163,000. ("Flipped" is an investor term for buying and selling right away.) It was a "cream puff" —two-story four bedroom, three bathroom, and three-car garage in a great area. Dawn didn't do anything to it. She bid on the nicest one on the HUD list and picked it up because there were no other bidders on the property.

Dawn says: "I guess I just lucked out. I loved buying properties and fixing them up; I also loved to work for myself. What freedom I had in my early years when all of my other friends had to work full time. Just like my Mom says 'carpet and paint makes you look like what you ain't', and 'there's bucks in yucks.' What someone would turn their nose up to, I bought and fixed up, and I said yuck all the way to the bank." (I love how Dawn says her "early years;" she is still a long way from thirty!) *Lesson learned: even a young single woman can transform houses for profit.*

Enicia's Home of Her Own

Our daughter Enicia and her husband Ted won the bid on a HUD home in Lake Elsinore. Real estate agents constantly tell us that we have to overbid by at least $20,000 to win the bid. Don't believe this! Enicia and Ted *underbid* on this property the day *after* bid closing. This was in 2003—not ancient history. When HUD doesn't get any bids, the property becomes a "daily," which means HUD accepts bids each day.

Not all HUD repos are fixers. Sometimes you get lucky bidding on HUD houses. Enicia and Ted's home didn't need paint, heavy cleaning, or new carpeting. Brian installed a new hot water heater, a dishwasher, and a garbage disposal. This property could have been immediately flipped for quick profit, but Enicia fell in love with the house and they decided to make it their own home.

After a few months, Enicia and Ted got a Home Equity Line of Credit and pulled $50,000 out to pay off debts and to buy another property. They turned a $5,000 down payment into $50,000 and paid less monthly for their mortgage than they would have for a rental apartment.

Through a family friend, Enicia and Ted located a bargain investment property—about thirty thousand under market—that came with excellent tenants who we know and no work required. Even if the real estate market loses its fast appreciation dynamic, their tenants will pay for the house and help finance our grandchildren's future education.

You too can make a fortune in real estate. During the past five years, our family has purchased over three million dollars worth of real estate, and we continue to look for our next investment property. We buy some properties to transform and sell for quick profit and we hold some properties for our future.

By writing this book, I hope to enable others to find financial success in real estate investing. Whether you desire more income for this year or for your retirement, enjoy the profit and potential financial freedom through transforming doghouses into dollhouses.

Chapter Two

Credit Help

Now that you know about the exciting possibilities in transformative real estate, you are probably anxious to get started. You must prepare for any real estate opportunity by obtaining financing first, so you are in the position to buy a bargain when you find one. Before we cover the more exciting information on how to find and fix distressed properties, it's important to start with credit issues. By getting a jump-start on establishing good credit, you ensure your ability to purchase a home or investment property.

I know readers get bored with technical information. Please keep this in mind: your quest for financial independence requires this crucial information. If you know *positively* that your credit score exceeds 720 and your income abundantly qualifies you for a new mortgage considering your existing debt, skip to Chapter Three. Otherwise, read and apply the information in this chapter to prepare yourself for incredible financial progress!

Establish Good Credit

You need at least three credit accounts to begin your credit history. Try to get credit accounts viewed favorably by mortgage lenders like bank credit cards and avoid consumer loans such as finance companies, department stores, and installment loans.

To help our eighteen- year-old son Kirk establish credit, I co-signed an auto loan. He applied for a Visa card through his college and another Visa card online. I pay him $1,500 a month. He pays a house payment for me, and makes his car and Visa payments. This gives him "stated income," a bank checking account, and a credit history, along with the ability to purchase property.

Married Couples
If you are married, establish separate credit accounts. Try to finance in just one partner's name to increase your investment financing potential. Avoid total joint account credit; the accounts in one partner's name only count against that individual's credit report. In other words, when applying for a loan, all of the accounts won't be listed as monthly expenses and this makes it easier to qualify for a loan. When beginning your investment business, keep in mind that double income qualifies for more.

Credit Checks and Reports

Before you begin your property search, **check your credit**. You need to know what is on your credit report—even if you think your credit is perfect. I thought my credit was perfect. What a shock to find out otherwise! If you have no credit—obtain your report anyway so you get into the system.

Order your credit report copy from all the major companies: Experian, TransUnion, and Equifax. You are entitled to one free report each year. You can go online and pay for an instant credit report.

Every time you apply for credit, ask to see your report and get the current contact information for the agency. I noticed that credit bureaus often change their toll–free telephone numbers answered by a live person. Check our website at www.recredithelp.com for the latest contact information.

To avoid charges, write to the following credit reporting agencies. Include your name, current address, last address, social security number, and birth date. Save time by including copies of your social security card, driver's license, and a utility bill proving your address. Otherwise, they might reply with a letter requesting this information and delay your credit report copy.

If the reporting agency already has a file on you at your present address, you may not need to provide these copies again. However, we have been asked for this information several times while living at the same address, even after they sent us reports at the same address. Since the bureaus behave so erratically, I can't promise how they will treat you. It depends on your urgency to get started and how you decide to handle your requests.

Credit Reporting Agencies
Experian
http://www.experian.com
701 Experian Parkway
P.O. Box 2002
Allen, TX 75013

TransUnion
http://www.transunion.com
TransUnion Consumer Relations
P.O Box 1000
Chester, PA 19022

Equifax
http://www.equifax.com
Equifax Credit Information
P.O. Box 740241
Atlanta, GA 30374

Sample letter format to obtain free credit reports:

> Name
> Social security number
> Birth date
> Address
>
> Credit report agency
> Address
>
> Date
>
> Dear Sir or Madam:
>
> Please send me a free copy of my credit report.
> Enter your reasons: [I have not received a copy from you
> within the last year. I have been denied credit from....I may

have to pay extra for a home loan because of misinformation in your report. I think there may be fraud using my name and my credit. I have reason to believe that certain information on your file is incorrect, such as…]

I need this immediately as I am buying a home [for my family].

Enclosed are the following documents: Copy of birth certificate and/ or driver's license, copy of social security card, copy of utility bill verifying address.

Thank you,

Signature
Your name

The reason that you need to obtain all your credit reports is to make sure that all the information is correct. If your credit history is excellent and correct and you have no room for improvement, you still need to find out your credit score.

Your free credit report does not give you your credit score; you either pay an extra fee for this information or ask a lender to run your credit for you. Credit scores will be covered in depth later in this chapter.

Once your reports arrive, create a file for keeping your credit reports, records, copies of letters, receipts of paid bills in dispute, and copies of dispute forms returned to credit agencies. Also write a letter to each agency listing a disputed item. Write individual letters for each disputed item if you have more than two complaints because the bureaus tend to bunch together items and not respond to each.

Sample Dispute Letter:

Name
Social security number
Birth date
Address

Complaint Department
Credit report agency
Address

Date

Dear Sir or Madam:

I am writing to dispute the following item in my credit report. Please note item encircled on the attached copy of the report I received.

[Identify item disputed by assigned identification number and by name of source, (such as creditors or tax court, and identify type of item, such as credit account, judgment, etc.)] is [inaccurate or incomplete] because [describe what is inaccurate or incomplete and why]. I am requesting that the item be deleted [or request another specific change] to correct the information.

Enclosed are copies of [describe any enclosed documentation, such as payment records, court documents]. Please delete or correct the disputed item immediately as I am financing a home.

Thank you,

Signature

Your name

Enclosures: [List what you are enclosing]

Credit Scores: Three Little Numbers that Cost or Save You Big Money

When you buy real estate, the lenders run all of the "big three" credit bureau reports. Each credit reporting agency lists your credit history as supplied to them by the individual lenders and includes governmental records. Each report assigns a credit score number to you. The credit scores reflect your theoretical risk of default to the lending institutions. Software developed by Fair Isaac and Company generates your "FICO score."

Experian uses a system called Fair Isaac Risk Model, a computer program which rates you with a score according to Experian's information. Equifax bases scores on BEACON programs and TransUnion bases scores on EMPIRICA models.

How Real Estate Lenders Rate You

Credit score	Available mortgage financing
720-800	Superb! You get what you want
700-719	Wonderful! You get top rates & terms
680–699	Good! You get good rates & terms
660-679	All right. You pay higher costs & rates
640-659	Okay. You need good income
620-639	Weak. You need good income & some money
600-619	Poor. Use creative loan broker & pay more
580-599	Almost impossible without large down payment
Under 580	Work on fixing credit without delay

Five Elements of Your Credit Score

Depending on the length of your credit history, you are rated on five categories representing percentages of your total credit score. Notice how the different categories weigh differently and which areas you have the most control over. Although there are ways to influence your past credit history, it is easier to manage the other factors. After discussing credit scores in depth, we will discuss how to fix credit issues.

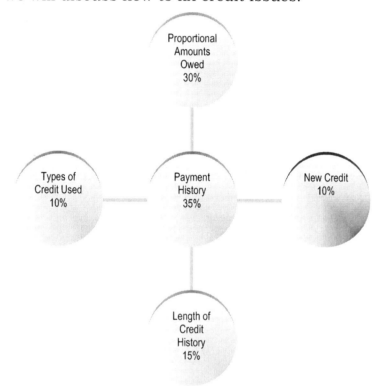

1.   Proportional Amounts Owed—30%

The amount owed on a credit line compared to the available credit is termed the proportional amount owed. With a credit card limit of $5,000, the score will be higher if less than $2,500 is owed. Even better is to owe less than 1/3rd of the available credit or less than $1501. To have the highest proportional amounts owed scoring factor, owing less than ten percent of the available balance gives you the best possible rating. On the other hand, owing over $4,500 on an account with a limit of $5,000 lowers your score significantly, especially if you have too many credit cards and other loans with high balances compared to available balances.

To raise your credit score dramatically and quickly, pay down as much as possible on each credit line instead of paying off one credit card at a time. If a credit card is totally paid off, it does not compute in the proportional amount owed; therefore your rating does not benefit from paying balances in full. On the contrary, paying balances in full takes the account out of the equation and you don't get higher points for the low proportional amount owed.

2.   Payment History—35%

Never, ever pay a mortgage payment more than 30 days late. Lenders do not like to see any delinquencies on real estate loans. Negative points lower credit scores because of any debt paid 30 days, 60 days, or 90 days late. The dollar amount of these delinquencies also impacts credit scores. Severity of delinquency, how long past due, and number of delinquencies determine nasty remarks on credit reports. The older these derogatory items are, the less impact they have on credit scores. You do not want any present delinquent accounts when applying for a loan.

On the other hand, the number of accounts paid as agreed and a good payment history give you a higher score.

Adverse public records, such as bankruptcy, judgments, suits, liens, and wage attachments negatively dominate credit history. Any of these items cleared up helps improve a credit score, *unless* the item is aged. The older the derogatory item, the less its impact. Any activity on a particular item makes the item update and therefore remain on the report for another *seven* years. Therefore, if a derogatory item is more than four or five years old, leave it alone.

Collection items unfavorably shape credit payment history. Again, the older a collection account is, the less its consequence. Most mortgage companies require that collection accounts be cleared before lending. If this is your problem—see "Help with Collections" later in this chapter.

3.   Length of Credit History—15%

Six months is the minimum length of time to establish credit. Any account over twelve months with a good payment history helps a credit score if the balance is not too high compared to the available credit. The time since accounts opened and the time since account activity are factored into the length of credit history. If you close any accounts, close the newest accounts and keep those with the longest history.

4.   New Credit—10%

Whenever you apply for a new credit line, your score receives a negative hit. The more inquiries you generate, the lower your score. Obtaining new credit lowers your credit score. We only apply for credit when applying for mortgages. Every time we get a new mortgage, our credit scores go down.

Never, ever finance a new car or get a new line of credit when you are getting ready to finance property. Wait until after closing to apply for further financing. Be aware that after your new loan shows up on your credit report, your financing abilities shrink. If you need credit funds for any reason, including renovation costs for your doghouse, apply for this the day after closing your property purchase.

5.   Types of Credit Used—10%

The different types of loans taken out by consumers affect credit scores. Credit assessors view mortgage accounts more favorably than consumer finance accounts. Too many installment loans, auto loans, and department store credit cards affect credit negatively.

To improve your credit score, pay off installment loans and consumer finance company accounts after you have lowered your proportional amounts owed. Then pay off your department store retail accounts. Keep balances as low as possible on home equity lines of credit because they often count as consumer finance accounts instead of mortgages. Achieve higher credit scores by having only mortgage accounts and a couple of major credit cards with low balances.

Your Baseline

You have three credit scores, often called FICO scores, one from each credit bureau. The lender takes the middle score as your baseline. Lenders have different standards, but generally a "C" score is around 500 to 600, a "B" is around 600 to 680, and an "A-" is above 680. Over 700 is the magical number that gets you the attention you desire. If your score is under 500, find someone to privately finance for you or a partner with good credit while you work on improving your score.

Do you need a credit score of 700? Don't believe it! We have so many loans; our scores are in the mid 600s, but we buy and sell all the time. Even with a perfect payment history, we can't get our scores up because we have so many real estate loans with high balances remaining. We usually have to get "B" loans instead of "A" loans, which means we pay higher tax-deductible interest, points, and fees.

Why Credit Scores Give False Impressions

A bank President, who is a member of our extended family, said the highest FICO score he ever saw belonged to a young woman with one credit card. The account, in perfect standing with a low balance, was twenty years old. Her parents had added her name to their account.

Kirk, our son attending college, has a credit score close to 800, yet he has no job! We pay all his bills; his credit score should be ours. This makes credit scores ridiculous to me. If lenders believe that the credit score reflects one's risk involved in paying back the mortgage, I don't understand why they don't give more recognition to borrowers who never miss a payment.

Improve Your Credit Score Yourself

Credit Repair Companies and Credit Counseling

Paying someone to "fix" your credit is a waste of your money. The negative issues temporarily dropped from your file just reappear in a couple of months. Mortgage brokers give the best advice for credit disputes and problems because they desire to help you finance property. Use them as your free credit counselors.

Be careful with credit repair scams.

Most of these companies really don't help and you can improve your credit more effectively on your own. **Credit counselors** promise to get you out of debt, not improve your credit report. Some of these companies have you send them one check a month and pay your creditors for you. What many do is pay your bills late. So your report becomes filled with "over 30 days late" notations and your credit score drops severely.

"Debt negotiators" posing as non-profit organizations ruin credit even worse. They advise people not to pay credit card bills at all.

Furthermore, they charge an upfront fee, a maintenance fee, and monthly fees. Then they collect money on a monthly basis and put it in a "trust" account. After a long time, debt negotiators get creditors to settle for less than owed as an "uncollectible account." This totally ruins credit, with many "over 90 days late" remarks and paid collections. Plus, all the so-called money saved—money really owed—is considered income by the IRS! In other words, if you owe $20,000 and settle for $12,000, you are required to list the $8,000 as income.

Battling the Big Three

I did all the steps suggested by my different lenders. I denied all negative remarks on the forms supplied by the credit bureaus. I wrote individual letters regarding each negative issue and supplied proof when needed. I kept copies of all documents in my "credit repair" file. The letters were in my computer so that I could re-date them and resend them again and again. I have been doing this for over *ten* years and they still have misinformation on our reports. Not once in all this time have the credit bureaus sent me a copy of my credit report that was completely accurate.

The hardest conflict we encountered with the credit reporting agencies was their confusing our credit with one of our son's. Because it looks like we have many more mortgages, credit cards, student loans, and car loans than we really do, our credit scores are inaccurate. I contacted our son's creditors as well as the credit bureaus. I am constantly fighting this battle. Some of our son's information drops off for awhile just to pop up again months later.

We hired an attorney to help us with our credit issues. The attorney effectively saved us thousands of dollars on loan costs—well worth the $595 investment.

The important lesson for you is that if we, with unfair low credit scores, can still buy property— so can you!

Help With Collections

Leave old uncollected bills alone because they will drop off your credit report eventually. Also, as these derogatory bills "age," they decrease in negative points. Paying old accounts off causes them to update to current information on your report and actually *increases* the negative points. As stated previously, any activity on an old bill will keep the account information on your credit report for another seven years. For instance, a forgotten bill from four years ago has few negative points. The same bill, if paid, becomes a current "paid collection" with more negative points, loses the four year age, and remains an additional seven years on the credit history.

If a lender requires that you clear all unpaid collection accounts, you can often get the original company to settle for half, as this amount is what they would get from a collector and they may feel that you will never pay anyway. Remember, any discount on your bill is "income" to you according to the IRS.

Paying the original company benefits you in two ways. First, you avoid painful dealings with collectors. More importantly, you maintain a better credit score by circumventing collectors. I refuse to settle with collection agencies because they report collections for seven years on credit histories after payment. If your credit report lists a collection agency, identify the original lender and deal directly with them. Call the initial company and ask them to settle for half. Any serious payment makes many of these companies happy. Make them promise to send you a receipt saying the account is settled in full and you owe them no more money. Get them to agree to remove any negative remarks from your credit report. Have them fax or mail you a letter agreeing to these terms before you send them payment—otherwise they may go back on their word. This works best if you promise to call back immediately with your credit card payment once you receive their fax or letter.

After settling, send a copy of the paid receipt to the collection agency and request they drop their report to the credit reporting bureaus who list this item. Because the original creditor settled, you do not owe the collector. Then fill out the credit bureau report form denying the bill and send them proof of payment to the original creditor.

Many creditors will not talk to you about the debt. They refer you to the collector. Don't be intimidated and do not call the collector unless you are prepared for a verbal battle. Calling collectors accomplishes little for you. If the initial company refuses to discuss your bill, send them a check anyway with a copy of the bill and note the account number on your check. Keep a copy of the check and bill in your credit file. Ask the bank for a check copy as you need the back of the check with paid information.

We were surprised to see many little collections on our credit report for medical bills we thought were covered by insurance. I found that if I sent checks directly to the original creditors, they all accepted payments. Then I sent copies of the checks to the credit bureaus. I filled out the credit bureau forms denying these collections and sent letters to the collection agencies refuting the debt. These collections disappeared from our credit reports.

Collection Agencies
Collection agencies often agree to settle for as little as ten percent of the amount billed. Collectors get paid by commission only when they receive payment and this means they want to get paid something over nothing. They get more motivated near the end of the month so this time-frame gives you more leverage.

Be wary of collectors promising to "delete" or list the account as "paid as agreed." Collectors, notorious for harsh manners and unethical collection practices, scam many struggling borrowers into paying and then break verbal promises to help clean up credit. Get collector promises in writing. Avoid "paid collection" listed on your credit report for seven more years.

Manage Debt with Credit Scores in Mind

Beneficial Method to Pay Credit Down

Raising the "proportional amounts owed" factor in your score uplifts your credit rating quickly. This factor contributes thirty percent of your overall credit score, and you possess the ability to change this portion easier than changing your credit history.

Being maxed out on credit cards damages your credit score. It is best to owe only 30% of the available credit on each card rather than to pay off the highest interest card first. The priority here is not getting out of debt by paying now. The priority is getting out of debt by making money to pay off all your bills through real estate profits. Imagine being able to write out checks paying off all your bills in one sitting! To improve your credit scores, pay as much more as possible instead of the minimum amount due.

There is another significant reason to make more than the minimum payment. Did you know that if you have around $21,000 in credit card debt, which is common in the United States, and 19.8% interest (also common) and you *quit* charging on these cards—it will take you *45 years* to pay off the debt if you only make minimum payments! Approximately *eighty percent* of these payments goes to interest only! That's over $41,000 in non-tax deductible interest alone.

Your goal is to pay down all your credit cards to less than 50%—30% is better—of the available credit owed on each card. Except for department store cards, do not close paid-off credit card accounts. In fact, for your real estate purchasing power, it is better to use a balance transfer from a paid-off card to an account with a higher balance. If you make a large payment on a credit card, the credit card company may increase your credit limit, which decreases your debt ratio, thereby improving your credit score. This is great if you don't use the available credit at this point. Wait until you are fixing up your doghouse!

Always pay house payments on time. A late mortgage payment hurts your credit history more than a late auto loan payment or late credit card payments. Lenders look more closely at real estate loans than at all other credit history.

Do not apply for more credit if you already have credit. Credit reporting bureaus list how many times you apply for credit as a negative. Every time you apply for credit, it deducts points from your score. Inquiries stay on your report for two years. Don't apply for unnecessary credit and don't make a major purchase—especially when you are in escrow—because you could lose your loan.

You can avoid negative remarks on your credit file if you work with your creditors instead of ignoring them when you have a cash flow emergency. Most credit companies allow you to skip a payment or to pay only a small amount towards interest, *if* you call them and make payment arrangements *before* the due date. Auto loans usually can be rolled over once a year. If you call your auto loan company and request that your payment be added to your account, be sure that they will not report it as being late. Most department stores let you skip a payment once or twice a year without reporting any negative, if you call before the due date.

"Too Much Consumer Credit" is a common remark listed on credit reports. Accounts with department stores, personal loans with finance companies, and other high interest, low-quality consumer loans affect the "Types of Credit Used," and these types of credit negatively impact credit.

Raising Credit Scores Quickly

It usually takes time to improve your credit score. You may need to pay higher mortgage interest rates and more loan costs starting out. However, there are some steps which show an immediate improvement.

We discovered we could raise our credit score by about 120 points by paying all our credit cards down to low balances. So, we put a no-cost home equity line of credit (HELOC) on a rental, and then paid down all credit cards and paid off all consumer loans. By not taking the full amount available—less than 50%—of the HELOC, our scores jumped 60 points in two weeks!

Report Large Payments
Remember to call the credit reporting agencies after you make large payments or pay off a consumer loan. Reporting these payments helps to speed up your credit score improvement. Most credit cards and loan companies report once a month to the credit bureaus. I found that contacting the credit agencies to report a large payment works faster because they request an update from the creditors. Otherwise, credit card companies and consumer lenders only report this information when they make their periodic report to the credit bureaus.

How to Get a Credit Score Over 700
1. Pay mortgages on time
2. Make no more than 1 late payment of 30 days on a credit line—no late payments of 60 days or more
3. Keep credit cards balances under 10% of available credit
4. Have only two to four major credit cards
5. No collections
6. No charge offs
7. No recent bankruptcies
8. No liens
9. No recent repossessions

Go on a Debt Diet to improve your credit score and purchasing power. Leave all your credit cards at home. Don't go to the mall. Spend your free time looking at houses. Make a grocery list and stick to it. Eat before you go to the market.

You will find it easier than you think not to spend money unnecessarily and your credit card debt won't increase.

Decide on an extra amount to pay towards debts weekly or monthly. I call this additional sum my **"investment fund"** because its purpose is to help finance income property. I believe it's better to get out of debt first before putting money into a saving account. Savings accounts do not pay as much interest as the interest paid out on credit. You may choose to add monthly savings to your investment fund.

There are many budget plans. With over thirty thousand diets to lose weight, I propose the following debt diets, which differ according to need.

Debt Diet to Raise Credit Scores
Split your investment fund and use this to pay two credit card accounts over the amount normally paid. Pay companies with high balances compared to open credit available. This reduces the proportional amounts owed factor, which is thirty percent of your credit score.

- Monitor credit line increases. Make use of account balance transfers to help pay off consumer finance companies.
- After all proportional amounts owed decrease to lower than 50%, pay down, with entire investment fund, one consumer finance account at a time.
- Pay off all consumer finance accounts. Roll each previous payment amount over into investment fund.

Your investment fund increases dramatically with each account paid off.

- Split increased investment fund and pay credit cards down to under 30% proportional amount owed.

- Use total investment fund to pay one high balance credit card down and ask for a credit line increase. Use balance transfer offers with lower interest to pay down consumer finance accounts. Keep records of when this low interest period ends and pay off the full amount prior to the ending date, or the lender may charge back interest for the entire amount.

- Pay down all credit cards to lower than 10% of proportional amount owed.

- Pay off all department store credit cards. If you have too much consumer credit, close department store credit cards.

- Close paid and unused accounts slowly over time; closing too many accounts at the same time lowers your credit score. Close out newest accounts first and keep those with longer credit history.

- Confirm that all closed accounts are reported as "closed by consumer" for the best report.

- Even if creditors offer to raise credit limits, allow only moderate credit limits.

- Keep your balances low and avoid revolving balances or open-end balances.

- **Add stability to your credit file** by keeping the same address, employment, and long term credit.

Debt Diet to Lower Debt-to-Income Ratio

Many times a borrower's problem is not credit, but too much monthly debt for available income. In these cases, apply the total investment fund to the lowest consumer or installment account balance first. This gets rid of the payment quickly and increases financing ability.

After you pay off the first account, add this payment amount to your investment fund. Pay the next account with the lowest balance off as quickly as possible with your increased investment fund. Keep rolling payment amounts of closed accounts into investment fund. This method reduces monthly payments and increases your financing abilities.

Careful Budgeting to Improve Credit Scores Doesn't Mean What Experts Advise

Against the advice of accountants who typically advocate paying off higher interest bearing accounts first, I believe in paying down debt differently. You can improve your credit score and financing abilities significantly if you carefully weigh all your alternatives.

If you are especially responsible, you can use your credit to your advantage. Make a huge payment on your Visa or Master Card at the beginning of the billing cycle. Include your normal grocery and gasoline budget. Use this credit card to pay for your *normal* expenses. Pay all these expenses off during the billing cycle *before* the charges and higher balances hit your credit report. What this can do for you is to increase your credit limit, thereby lowering your debt ratio and improving your credit score. This happens because the credit card companies believe large payments mean you can afford more credit.

Please be extremely careful doing this! You do not want to create more debt. Do not charge things you would not ordinarily purchase. One major problem with credit cards is that you don't hand over the money while shopping, and you become tempted to overspend.

Business Lines of Credit

We started a business in order to purchase our materials wholesale. I applied for credit cards in my company name using my social security number. The really beneficial outcome is that these accounts do not show up on my credit report! So, I use these credit accounts to purchase supplies and materials without negatively affecting my credit score.

To set up your business, file a fictitious business statement, (this is done at a local newspaper in California), apply for a city or county business license—and if required, a state tax ID number, and possibly a Federal ID number. You need enough documentation to open a business checking account and then you are prepared to apply for business credit.

Ready, set, go...

Your real estate business is a step-by-step process. After you receive your credit reports, work on any issues you uncover. Then you will be ready to begin your quest for financing and your search for distressed property. It is important to have your financing in place when you find the perfect investment opportunity.

Chapter Three

Financing Your Doghouse

Your financial opportunities do not depend solely on your credit history. You also need to understand your financing options and know what to look for in a lender. There are hundreds of loan programs from which to choose. This chapter contains important information and should not be overlooked even if it seems boring! Your expertise with financing, loan programs, and your particular mortgage needs will save you thousands of dollars and opens doors to your financial freedom.

Mortgage companies inundate homeowners with mailings that promise all kinds of unbelievable deals. When you understand this chapter, you will know what the fine print means, and you'll know how to get truly great financing options.

Types of Mortgage Lenders

With a middle credit score above 670 and sufficient income, almost any bank or **direct lender** will finance your purchase. A direct lender represents the bank or financial institution which funds the loan and uses loan officers to arrange financing. Loan officers working for banks do not need to have a mortgage broker's license and usually get paid a salary instead of commission.

Mortgage or loan Brokers originate over half of all mortgage loans. Loan brokers shop the banks and mortgage lenders, finding the best loan to suit your needs. With lower credit scores, you'll need to find an aggressive loan broker with a good closing record.

Lenders have different standards. Every bank and each lender has different rules. Your credit score is not the only factor considered. Some banks require higher income, more income documentation, and higher property standards.

Predatory Lenders

Most mortgage brokers provide good service to their clients, yet a few use unethical practices. These brokers, termed "predatory lenders," not only over charge, but they get paid in hidden ways. Avoid predatory lenders who charge more than the usual three percent fees for a conventional loan and four percent fees for a government-sponsored loan. Even non-prime lenders can't justify excessive fees.

Watch for hidden costs, such as the **Yield-Spread Premium**. This term refers to a rebate given to brokers when they place a borrower in an interest rate higher than the rate for which they qualify. Identify and avoid these brokers and refuse to pay yield-spread premiums and unwarranted fees.

What Lenders Look For

Lenders control many programs—some individual lenders make use of over 200 load programs! Generally, lenders look for the following typical standards, with many exceptions:

1. Absolutely no late mortgage payments
2. Credit score above 580
3. If bankruptcy, no charge-offs or collection accounts afterwards
4. If bankruptcy, only 1 late payment afterwards
5. Two active revolving accounts in good standing
6. Good employment history or stated income
7. Three to six months reserves (covering mortgage payment, taxes & insurance) in savings
8. 55% income to debt ratio
9. Appropriate loan-to-value ratio on purchase property

Borrowers obtain a loan by bringing something of value to the table. *One* of the following assets ought to get you financing:

1. Good credit score
2. Good income
3. Good cash down payment and reserves

Seven Loan Types and Finance Terms

Understanding the variety of loan types and terms enables you to choose an effective lender. Here are seven important loan types and related terms:

1.   "A" Loans

Borrowers with great credit, a good cash reserve, good employment, and a debt-to-income ratio of less than 33%, qualify for "A" loans. These loans typically cost less upfront for points and costs, charge no prepayment penalty, and offer lower interest rates.

2.   Non-Prime Loans

Credit reporting agency websites portray Americans as having great credit. These informational articles and graphs mislead and cause struggling home buyers to feel inadequate. In fact, my Countrywide lending contact told me that 60% of all applicants are considered "sub-prime" borrowers. Non-prime borrowers usually have credit scores under 620 or other conditions such as undocumented stated income, poor employment history, or credit issues such as collections, charge offs, and late payments.

3.   Stated Income Loans

Most applicants for a mortgage have a full-time job with income tax returns verifying income for the past two years. Other borrowers, like me, with multiple streams of income must get loans with stated income. Some lenders require two years of bank statements showing deposits equaling the required total income, proving the ability to make the mortgage payment.

4.   Full-Documented Loans

These loans require tax returns, employment verification, bank statements, and other individual lender demands. Other processing types, more flexible and easier for the borrower to gather information for, do not necessarily cost more. High credit scores, big down payments, and large cash reserves ease documentation requirements.

5.   Conforming Loans and Jumbo Loans
According to Fannie Mae and Freddie Mac guidelines, "conforming loans" are mortgages for less than the following allowable amounts at the time of this writing:

(Unit= dwelling or housing unit)
1 unit $333,700
2 units $413,100
3 units $499,300
4 units $625,000

Note: the amounts are higher in Hawaii and Alaska. Other states like California, New York, and Florida join the higher limits this year. The dollar amount of these loans changes periodically.

Conventional lenders also use the term conforming loans for loans which are not Fannie Mae and Freddie Mac loans. The term conforming loans simply refers to the dollar amount; it doesn't mean you get a Freddie Mac or Fannie Mae loan.

6.   "Jumbo loans" are for higher dollar amounts. You need jumbo loans to finance properties requiring larger mortgages than the limited conventional loan amount. Jumbo loans usually charge higher interest rates than conforming loans.

7.   Home Equity Line of Credit (HELOC)

If you already own your own home, consider a Home Equity Line of Credit, with few fees and lower costs, for purchasing investment property. Use this line of credit for a large down payment on your investment properties over and over. With twenty percent or more down on an investment property, you get better and easier financing, and save thousands of dollars on loan costs.

Mortgage Finance Terms

Fair Market Value

The sales price a willing and able buyer will pay a seller who is not under pressure to sell.

Loan to Value Ratio

The LTV or Loan to Cost Ratio compares the fair market value of the property to the loan amount. This cushion amount tells the lender if potential losses due to foreclosure may be recouped by selling the property.

Reserves are funds in your bank accounts, either savings or checking, which should equal at least three monthly payments including **PITI**— principal, interest, taxes, and insurance.

PMI: Private Mortgage Insurance

When you have less than 20% of the purchase price as a down payment on a government-licensed company loan, such as Freddie Mac or Fannie Mae, you need to pay PMI, private mortgage insurance. Although not government-owned, the government highly regulates these loan corporations. PMI is supposed to be removed on a loan after the property value increases to an amount 20% higher than the loan or the mortgage is paid down to 80% loan-to-value. Not all low-down mortgages require PMI, but it is a typical requirement on a low interest "A" type loan.

PMI is not an income tax write-off. Many borrowers get an 80% first and a 15%-20% second to avoid PMI. Although it doesn't make much difference to the overall monthly payment, there is no PMI with this double loan and all the interest is tax deductible.

Note: this is a good reason to use non-prime loans. It is cheaper to pay higher tax-deductible interest than PMI.

Prepayment Penalty

With excellent credit, prepayment penalties should not be an issue, but many loans include extra prepayment costs. Ask your prospective lenders about their policy regarding paying off the loan during the first two or three years. You need not disclose that you intend to flip the property, but you need to know how much this will cost you. Some lenders charge six months of interest as a prepayment penalty, which quickly adds up to thousands of dollars. If you intend to sell your dollhouse right away, avoid prepayment penalties by paying higher monthly interest. A few hundred dollars extra in interest costs less than paying six months of interest.

Guard Your Money

Besides giving attention to prepayment penalties, you need to pay attention to points and other loan costs. Get lender statements listing points and costs up front. **Points** are the lender fees based on a percentage point of the loan amount. One point is common for loan brokers, but they may try to charge more by reminding you of your credit score. This is why you need to shop around.

Be wary of hidden costs, such as duplicate lender underwriting fees and lender processing fees. Some lenders add on additional miscellaneous fees often called "garbage fees." Look carefully at your good faith estimate and ask about the charges. Keep in mind: you possess the final word and it's up to you to negotiate the best deal.

The nonrecurring closing costs include escrow fees and loan costs, not prepaid taxes or fire insurance. Many lenders allow the seller to pay a portion of your nonrecurring costs. To save on out-of-pocket expenses, figure the total cash needed to close escrow and how to add some costs to the loan. Closing costs and loan costs can either be paid by the seller or added to the loan according to the lender's requirements. Obtain the best possible financing by understanding the percentage down required, whether or not you can finance closing costs, and if the lender allows the seller to pay a portion of your closing costs.

Lender's Appraisers

Ask your prospective lenders about their appraisers. You need a good appraisal for the maximum loan, not an appraiser who has a record of low-balling property. Some banks with easy loan qualifications regularly use appraisers who give low values. This protects the lending institution because they take back many properties and gain more profit when they previously undervalued the property.

Also, ask the lender if the condition of the property hugely impacts the appraisal. Steer clear of appraisers discounting heavily for cosmetic conditions, like paint and decorating and the overall lack of tidiness—circumstances often causing a lower purchase price but not necessarily reflecting property value.

Appraisers on Your Side

Hire your own appraiser first and then have your lender "review" your good appraisal. This circumvents the problem of low appraisals.

Health and Safety Codes

Many lenders refuse to finance uninhabitable houses. According to your lender's standards, health and safety codes require forethought. Look for houses needing only cosmetic work for easier financing. Research your local health and safety codes or ask your lender for specific requirements.

Sometimes the sellers will cooperate to bring a property up to basic health and safety standards.

Just a few dollars or a little work makes all the difference. The seller can re-attach and cover exposed wires and electrical outlets. Leaky roofs can be repaired or replaced in escrow and billed to the escrow account. California codes call for smoke detectors and earthquake straps securing hot water heaters.

Funding Time
Also inquire about lenders' normal time-frame for funding. Some financial institutions rush purchase loans through quickly, whereas other lenders push refinancing loans. Wells Fargo Bank promised purchase financing in one week, even during the month of their most loans funded ever (August, 2003).

How to Find a Great Loan Officer

Because you need quick action when applying for a purchase loan, find a loan officer who you can access easily. A lender's quick response signifies good service to follow.

The best way to find a good lender is to ask another investor for a referral. Also, escrow officers and real estate agents know loan officers who close loans efficiently in a timely manner. Avoid advice from agents or others who receive a kick-back commission for referring you, as you may pay for this referral with added charges to your loan. Once you find an outstanding loan officer, establish a long term relationship for repeat business and better service. Your lender is one of your most important connections.

Once you know your middle credit score, look for a lender appropriate to your specific needs. When ready to make offers to purchase, apply for credit. Choose at least three lenders to apply with and do it at the same time. Call all your prospective lenders during the same week. This counts as only one inquiry on your credit report. Credit bureaus expect borrowers to shop for a loan.

Lender's Checklist
Ask potential lenders about the following requirements and costs according to a price range you think matches your needs. This also helps determine what you need to look for in a property.

Qualifications
- Middle credit score
- Income required

Loan costs
- Points
- Processing fees
- Additional "garbage" fees (underwriting fees, loan documentation preparation fee, filing fees, credit report)
- Hidden costs
- Prepayment penalty
- Interest Rate
- PMI (mortgage insurance)
- Prepayment penalties
- Are loan costs added to loan or prepaid?
- Is the seller allowed to pay a percentage of nonrecurring closing costs for the borrower? What is the maximum allowable seller contribution?

Requirements

- Percentage of purchase price required down? Or loan to value ratio?
- What about the condition of the property? Do they finance "fixers"?

A Better Way to Find Your Lender

After you work through all the details of the lender's checklist, you understand better the available possibilities. Now, from a different point of view, work backwards. Instead of asking the lenders what they offer you—tell them what you want and find the lender who best matches *your* terms. Create your own wish list of your personalized loan needs.

Personalized Lender Checklist

- Is this purchase an owner-occupied or an investment property?
- What percentage do you want to put down?
- If you want to sell right away, can you avoid prepayment penalties?
- Do you need the loan to finance a fixer? How much of a fixer do you want to tackle?
- How flexible are the lender's appraisers? Do you need a cooperative appraiser?
- Do you care about "garbage fees" and need these to be added to the loan?
- Do you want PMI, or a first and a second, or neither?
- Do you want the seller to pay your closing costs? How much?
- How many points do you agree to pay upfront or add to the loan?
- Are super low payments available?

Make your own Lender Checklist according to your abilities and find the lender who comes closest to your needs. Remember, a good loan broker wants your business and works hard to find the right loan out of thousands to suit your requirements. However, asking a lender for impossible demands wastes both of your time. Notice the difference in loan requirements, loan costs, and lender's attitudes. Figure out your qualifications, your loan needs, and find a matching lender with first-class service.

Amazing Available Loan Possibilities

As a point of reference for possible financing, consider the amazing loan our lender found for us:

No money down—stated income—no prepayment penalty—easy qualifications
Does this sound too good to be true? No, this 100% purchase price loan of $128,000, in December 2003, came with an easy appraisal review and "fixer" property allowed. We added the closing costs to the purchase price of $125,000. Requirements:

1. Credit score above 680
2. Stated monthly income of $4,000
3. No bankruptcy in last 7 years
4. No late mortgage payments
5. 3 credit lines open with at least one open for 24 months with a minimum credit limit of $2,400
6. Prior mortgage or provable rent history
7. 2 months of PITI reserves (principle, interest, taxes, and insurance)

8. 50% debt to income ratio [debts include credit card payments, car payments, other mortgages, (including taxes and insurance), and payments on any other installment loans (boats, timeshares)]
9. Only a couple of late installment payments

You can't get away with any negative remarks on your credit report with this no-money-down loan. This was a fixed 7% thirty year loan with a balloon payment due in fifteen years. We have never kept a mortgage for fifteen years. The 1% higher interest only costs a couple of hundred dollars for the few months we planned to keep the property—a great bargain for no money down and no prepayment penalty!

Five Percent Down and Super Low Payments
Another amazing loan our daughter found came with an adjustable rate mortgage with payments locked at 1.25% interest for the first five years. Enicia's new loan for her rental property offers such low payments that she immediately receives a positive cash flow, a previous impossibility in California. The payments are amortized over forty years.

Closing or Escrow Officers
If you don't already have a friendly and experienced escrow officer, ask your lender for a referral. Lenders and escrow officers who value a working relationship help each other close loans and escrows efficiently. Build a positive relationship with your escrow officer so they work harder for you.

Escrow companies affiliated with a title insurance company save you money if they give a discount for doing both the title insurance and the escrow. This mostly happens when you sell because often the seller has the right to choose these services. Bring into play these useful contacts when buying directly from owners.

Ready to Find Your Investment Property

After your credit is in order and you have found a lender, you are now ready to seek your fortune in real estate. Prepared investors secure the bargain properties when they spot them because they previously arranged financing and act without delay.

Chapter Four

Finding Your Doghouse

Locating your best investment property for maximum profit takes time and planning. First, you need promotional materials to take with you as you learn your target markets. This step helps you find unlisted deals. Then you need to know where to look for what, how to calculate a property's potential profit, and how to make offers.

Promotional Supplies

Business Cards

Start with business cards matching your personality so people remember you by your card. If you are vibrant, make your card flamboyant. If you are a serious business person, make your card more serene. A photograph of yourself helps contacts remember you.

Say something simple on your cards like the frequently used, yet still effective, "I buy houses." Think of a catchy slogan to personalize your cards so they are remarkable. I use large print for those of us who refuse to wear our glasses all the time. Make use of the back of your business cards for additional information.

We Buy Houses

"Call us for a fair & fast sale!"

Brian & Jeanette Fisher
1 (800) 246-5161

Pass out business cards liberally to all real estate agents and to anyone who knows of a possible distress sale. Remain loyal to your real estate agent, but also use other agents who come up with a great deal. Don't limit your possibilities. Give your cards to all your friends and family and ask them to share them with everyone.

Postcards
Creative postcards with a fabulous scene or beautiful home on one side and your business information on the backside have longer staying power than ordinary business cards. Besides handing them out like business cards, you can also mail postcards to homeowners of vacant or rundown homes.

Flyers
Artistic flyers with different messages benefit you in many ways. Hand out flyers and hang them up on local bulletin boards.

Look for a cute cartoon or striking graphic to make your flyer attract attention. Try varying messages such as:

Family Home needed immediately
Handyman husband—any condition o.k.
Have loan in place
Call for quick action
Please help!

Investor wants property in this area
Full price for good terms
Can close escrow quickly
Any condition acceptable!

Thinking about selling your home?
We need a home in this neighborhood.
Call us for a fair offer today.
We have cash for a quick sale!

When looking for properties, pass out your cards and flyers in the neighborhoods that interest you.

Location

You still can buy a house in Marion, Kansas for $18,500 with no money down, but can you make any money on it?

On the other hand, if your local area is too expensive to begin your real estate business, go out of town to get your first house. Your major concern is to get a starter property. Consider outlying areas within an acceptable driving distance. Thoroughly check out the neighborhood before committing. Remember...Location, Location, Location.

Look for areas and neighborhoods where there is a wide spread of housing prices and room for larger profits. Newer tract house developments with little pricing spread usually don't have enough room to make a profit. We find the easiest moneymakers in areas with all types of houses. We specialize in an area in Southern California where houses sell from $150,000 to $350,000. We look for houses around $150,000 that we fix up to sell for $225,000 or more.

Second Homes
Purchasing a second home in an area you take pleasure from achieves two benefits. You get to enjoy mini vacations while working on your doghouse and you take advantage of easier financing with lower down payments by purchasing the home as an owner-occupant second home.

Price
Don't buy expensive homes and expect a quick profit. It takes longer to sell a higher priced property in most areas because you limit the number of available buyers. The exception to this may be markets such as Los Angeles and Orange County, California, where buyers compete for properties and bid over listed prices. Take care; the hot market in San Francisco crashed during the technology mini-crisis. Higher-end homes lose more value in hard times. These troubled homeowners sell to salvage some equity and vie for the less expensive homes. Therefore, the lower priced homes maintain their value. People always

need housing and there are more buyers in the lower price range.

The exception to this principle is, with sufficient cash reserves, you make more on a $250,000 home in a $400,000 to $500,000 neighborhood. Some investors specialize in these types of properties. One couple in our area buys $300,000 homes on large pieces of land and turns them into estates worth $600,000 or more. They live in the property, fix it up themselves with outside help, and wait two years to sell to avoid capital gains tax.

Learn Your Market

Examine your chosen real estate market closely. Go to Open Houses. Call for information on FSBOs ("fisbos" or for sale by owners.) Explore your local and possible second home locations. Pick up real estate flyers and keep a file with housing prices and notes about the properties so you can watch trends. Call the listing agents representing the homes. Make records and follow your target areas, watching sales. Note which houses sell quickly, their sales price, and their conditions. With financing in place, jump when you uncover a great deal.

Many avenues exist for you to find your investment property. Keep researching your target market areas and passing out your cards and flyers. Follow newspaper ads, web information, and find agents to uncover bargain houses for you. Don't limit your possible leads with only one method of finding your doghouse.

How to Select a Real Estate Agent

Asking other investors for a good agent referral is a good place to start. Other ways to find good agents include asking your lender or finding your personal agent on your own. Agents representing the seller must give their clients the advantage; therefore look for an agent to represent you as the buyer. *Buyer's agents* specialize in negotiating the best deals for their clients. Seek out professionals by visiting open houses or calling from a referral or an advertisement.

Telephone Contact

Keep in mind: real estate agents take turns answering the phones, therefore, your first contact telephone call masks the response time of the agent returning calls. If you reach an agent the first time, don't expect that kind of constant service.

Busy real estate agents try to monopolize your first contact to qualify *you* when you need to qualify the agent. Look for:

- Ease of contact
- Cooperation
- Knowledge of area and real estate law
- Recent active sales
- Knowledge of HUD and VA procedures
- Agents not overwhelmed with investors
- Creative and positive attitude
- Experience or willingness to learn
- Good track record of closing sales

Do not sign an agreement with any real estate agent limiting you. Many agents want you to sign a contract promising to pay them a commission—even if you buy a "for sale by owner"! You want to use many agents in many areas. Tell the agents that you look for multiple properties and use multiple sources for finding great deals.

Secure your lender before you make offers. At this point, tell your real estate agents that you qualify to buy a property from them when they present you with a great deal. Give the agent your lender's name and phone number. This proves your seriousness and amplifies your attention from the agent.

Know Yourself

Understand your capabilities and limits. You want challenges and learning experiences teaching you new methods of transforming a doghouse into a dollhouse. However, don't buy a decrepit house that needs way more than you know how to do, unless you know how much professionals charge to do the difficult work and possess sufficient funds to cover this work.

Perhaps working overtime at your job and paying helpers less money for the time spent will save you money. Think about the work involved in cleaning, repairing, and decorating. Will this be fun or torment to you? Because I love transforming a junky house into a palace, I would rather pay a housekeeper to clean my own home while I scrub walls and clean toilets in my future dollhouse.

Estimating Transformation Costs

Before you make an offer on a good deal, formulate a worksheet estimating out of pocket expenses. You limit your profit potential when you pay too much for a house that needs too many costly repairs. For complete estimating worksheets see *Doghouse to Dollhouse for Dollars Workbook.*

The following is our estimating worksheet for an average three bedroom home:

1.	Paint, interior & exterior	$100-500
2.	Carpeting	$1,000-4,000
3.	Flooring	$300-3,000
4.	Repair or new roof	$400-2,500
5.	Heating & air conditioning	$300-2,000
6.	Appliances	$335 each
7.	Hot water heater	$250
8.	Lighting fixtures	$5-100 each
9.	Ceiling fans	$50-150 each
10.	Toilets	$75-150 each
11.	Sinks	$50-150 each
12.	Landscaping	$50-300
13.	Miscellaneous	$1,000

The following costs vary according to the property:
1. Monthly mortgage
2. Utilities
3. Outside help
4. Price of property

5. Closing costs (points, prepaid interest, fire insurance, loan
    costs, and escrow fees)
    Estimated Expense Total

Estimated Value after Transformation

Selling costs (usually about 8% of selling price)
Estimated time (number of mortgage payments)
Total expenses and costs
Estimated Sales Price
Profit potential

Lower Your Initial Expenses

Include estimated renovation costs in your offer to
purchase. If beginning your real estate investment
business, think about asking the seller to fix or
replace high-ticket items like the roof and the
heating and air conditioning systems in escrow.
Ask the seller to pay your closing costs and ask
for a rebate of cash for other fix-up costs. If
necessary, increase the purchase price to cover
part of these expenses. See "making offers" for
more information. Adding these costs to the
purchase price lowers your upfront costs, but
higher loan costs decrease your profit potential.

Calculate out-of-pocket expenses and know
where these funds will come from. Many
companies offer promotions with no interest and
no payments for a year. Home Depot and Lowe's
frequently give credit for three to twelve months
with no interest charges. (Apply for Home Depot,
Lowe's and other home improvement warehouse
credit *after* you close on your doghouse escrow.
Better yet, apply in your new business name.)

Coupons Save You Transformation Costs

Both Home Depot and Lowe's usually send a nice coupon for 10% off to your newly purchased home address. We wait for this coupon to purchase appliances and other large ticket items. Typically, both companies accept each other's coupons. Unfortunately, most of these coupons take too long to come for you to wait to get started on your doghouse.

Types of Properties to Find

To make a good profit in real estate, you must buy right. Check out all property types available to find the best transaction for your specific situation. Consider fixers, distressed sales, repossessions, multiple listings, for sale by owners, and vacant properties just wasting away.

Distressed Properties

Recognize the difference between a fixer and a distressed property. Distressed properties may be fixers or just unwanted houses. Divorce, job loss or transfer, death, financial difficulty, and other problems often force a sale for less than market value. Just because an owner's problem causes a distressed sale does not mean the house requires a lot of repair.

Repossessions

Look for great bargain properties for sale by HUD, VA, Freddie Mac, Fannie Mae, and Bank-REOs (acronym for real estate owned). Real estate agents try to discourage you from repos and

switch you to multiple listed homes. Do not listen
to negative remarks about how hard it is to find a
good deal property. Find another agent. Even in
the hot market at the time of this writing, when
the average house sells in less than three weeks,
we found two properties for at least forty
thousand dollars under market value.

**Paying a listing service to mail you lists of
repossessed properties is a waste of money.**
Actually, by the time you get these lists, the
houses are already sold. Many web sites listing
foreclosures thrive on the web for no charge to
you. See www.doghousetodollhouse.com for updated
foreclosure links.

Take a flashlight with you to view a repossessed
property. These houses have no electrical service
and boards covering windows. A good real estate
agent will have her own flashlight, but you want
to see what you want and not what she wants you
to see.

HUD
In our area, new HUD listings post online late
Thursday night or Friday morning. New "Daily's,"
homes previously sold which fell out of escrow,
post Saturday morning. Properties not sold
during the bid time stay listed as daily's. Bids,
due by the following Tuesday at midnight, must
be submitted by a real estate agent who has
completed HUD registration.

Find an agent specializing in HUD homes who
wants to work with you on your terms. Don't

waste your time using a Realtor who is not familiar with selling HUD homes. Any mistake causes the bid to be rejected. Don't use an agent who says you must bid way over minimum bid. Many bargain HUD homes do sell for far more than the minimum bid. Hold out for the one property which doesn't get way overbid. (I bid about $40,000 *under* minimum in 2001 on our second home owner-occupant mountain cabin.)

We submit many bids and win enough to make it pay us well. HUD only allows one repo purchase as an owner-occupant every two years from the date of closing. This is why we split our purchasing power. My husband buys one, I buy one, our daughter buys one...

Rely on your gut instinct and don't let your real estate agent unduly influence you. It is not a difficult process for your agent to make a computer bid. You need an agent willing to make a few bids to get a successful bid. This is like winning a lottery, with the odds in your favor.

Bids must have a lender's loan commitment statement. Lenders unfamiliar with HUD requirements also waste your time. Any mistake causes you to lose the purchase. Not all lenders understand HUD's bid, finance, and purchase process.

When placing a HUD bid, raise your offering bid to cover some of your closing costs. This means you get HUD to pay your closing costs and save out-of-pocket expenses. Also, the higher sales price impacts the market comparable sales in your favor for sale later. Your purchase price influences the values of the market area. Keeping prices higher for active sales during your renovation time protects your investment potential.

Don't get attached to one particular property. We placed a bid on a home I loved in Apple Valley and lost it by a few hundred dollars. The house came back on the list later, not at all uncommon for HUD repos. But by this time, we had already purchased a better distressed property.

VA

Cleaner than HUD repos, homes owned by the Veterans Administration are also offered on a bidding system through real estate agents. The VA partially fixes up their repossessed homes. Lists of available VA properties online show photos and virtual tours. The VA sometimes offers vendee (seller) financing with few processing costs, low interest, and no prepayment penalty. You do not have to be a Veteran to buy these easy-to-qualify for homes.

As of this writing, the VA is changing the way these homes are offered for sale. This is another reason you need a real estate agent who stays on top of recently revised marketing procedures relating to government-owned properties.

Less-known government agencies such as Fannie Mae, Freddie Mac, FDIC, SBA, the IRS, and GSA, list repossessed properties on their individual web sites. These properties, more rare than HUD and VA, usually get cleaned and repaired before listing with real estate agencies with sale prices closer to market value.

REOs

Banks often offer their real estate owned—REO homes at bargain prices. Depending on the bank's resale policy, conditions of the property, and available financing, REO opportunities vary widely. Several banks lend on their repos while other banks just want out. Great financing becomes possible through banks that offer in-house terms. Ask for no points, minimal loan costs, and no prepayment penalties. Check with your local lending institutions and find out how they market their repossessions. Many of these bankers will give you their web page listing available property. Befriend real estate agents who specialize in listing bank-owned repossessions so they will notify you of a new listing immediately.

Multiple Listings

It is hard to find a bargain in multiple listings, but not impossible. Check out listings which have been on the market for awhile. Look for vacant houses because these cost the seller money every month. Make an offer for much less than asking price with a quick escrow. Many anxious sellers jump on an offer if they think they will be out of their problem in only ten days. This is another reason you need a lender and an escrow officer who perform fast.

I follow the multiple listings in our area on the Multiple Listing Service. One of my agents emails me new listings daily. You need an agent who calls you the minute a new distressed property listing becomes available. Under-priced listings usually get snapped up by the real estate agents and their investors before they hit the market.

Just like making many bids, make many offers. You never know when a seller's problems reach a critical point causing abrupt action.

For Sale by Owners

Houses for sale by owner may not always be a great buy, but there is always at least one bargain out there. Many investors prefer buying directly from the owner. If you have ever tried to sell your home by yourself, you probably met some of these investors. Investors working out of self-interest, and in some cases fraudulent, dream up all kinds of schemes to buy houses from distraught homeowners at the lowest possible cost. Understand that the home seller most likely dealt with these callous investors before you and therefore may view you with suspicion. Earn sellers' trust by working with them honestly and compassionately.

Seller's Motivation

Let honesty and kindness guide your actions with sellers. Finding out the seller's specific problem is the key to helping them and yourself. Uncover the seller's particular need and find a solution. Because it's embarrassing for some sellers to let you in on their troubles, extra sympathy and relaxed timing helps you unearth their underlying motivation. Listen carefully, *stop talking*, and pay attention to details which lead to understanding the real reason they need to sell.

The seller may need a quick escrow, need to rent back the home for a while, or want immediate cash. You could give the seller a loan of cash with a note secured by the property. Ask an attorney about your state laws regarding this type of purchase advance. We offered a seller a $2,000 deposit outside of escrow, which went toward the down payment, to entice a money-hungry seller to commit to our low price.

Many sellers do not need all of their cash out. Owner financing is a great deal for you. Usually, you get a lower interest rate and you don't have to pay lender's points or prepayment penalties. Also, these loans typically won't show on your credit report so you won't have these payments counted against you. If you have a good credit report, take a copy with you to show to the seller. This prevents more inquiries on your credit history and prevents lowering your credit score.

Making Offers

When you look at homes for sale by owners, be polite about the condition. The seller knows the faults of the property and won't care to be reminded of his or her failure to fix it up. Other investors before you most likely insulted the seller by complaining about the work required to fix up their mess. Always find something to compliment the seller on, even if it's just the setting.

Sellers think a quick agreement on sales price and terms means that they are a pushover. They like to take time in making a deal. After previewing the property and establishing a relationship with the seller, start the following repetitive questions and never offer your price or terms. Pause between questions. Learn to keep quiet, even when the silence hurts, and listen carefully.

What to Say to Sellers:

Say; "I understand how difficult it is for you. What's the best you can do so I can help you to move on?"

"What is the best you can do?"
"Is this really the best you can do?"
"If I made you an offer right now to close in 30 days, what could you do?"

Never make an offer until you go around again.
"What is the best you can do?"
"Is this really the best you can do?"
"If I made you an offer right now to close in 21 days, what could you do?"

And again...
"What is the best you can do?"
"Is this really the best you can do?"
"If I made you an offer right now to close in 10 days, what could you do?"

Insert another phrase instead of "close in ten days" relating to the seller's problems and needs.

Such as: "What if you could stay in the home for a few weeks or longer until you find a new home?" Or, "What if I could advance you some money today?" Offer a small deposit as an option to buy the property. Many desperate sellers are motivated by getting a few hundred dollars immediately. You can write up the contract with the option to purchase money becoming part of the down payment. We purchased Valley View Ranch with a $2,000 deposit check to the seller, which he cashed without delay.

Write up your sales contract listing sales price. Always come prepared with your real estate purchase contract, or pen and paper. A simple contract stating seller's and buyer's names, property address, sales price, deposit receipt payable to escrow, and date of sale works to open escrow. We left off the termite report clause on our last purchase and this helped to avoid repair issues with the lender because we purchased the property "as is."

Conditions in Your Offer
Once you finish the first part of the sales contract, your seller relaxes. At this point, **chip away at the sales price or expenses** to you. Ask the seller to reduce the price, according to a real estate fee. Say, "I get compensated for my work handling the escrow company and finding financing much like a real estate agent. I'll cut the normal fee in half for you. OK?" Perhaps you get a three percent price reduction just for asking.

Ask for a big discount for a fast escrow. Say, "If I can move the closing date sooner for you to get your money faster, will you help me with my first monthly payment?"

The seller tires of saying "no" to everything. If you get no cooperation on further price reduction or cash back to you, ask for the appliances. Say, "Will you help me out by leaving the heavy refrigerator? It's so hard to move and I need one." Pause. "What about the stove? They usually come with the property."

Continue with repairs made in escrow and ask about the roof, the termite repairs, carpeting, hard flooring, and new dishwasher. For "Making Offers Checklist" see *Doghouse to Dollhouse for Dollars Workbook.*

If the doghouse is in serious need of a roof, ask for this to be done in escrow. If the seller won't pay for this, you can increase the sales price to cover the roof costs and have this amount added to your loan. Be sure to specify the type and brand of roof or "buyer's choice of roof up to dollar amount" in your contract.

If the seller balks at paying for the roof, say, "All right, I'll pay for the roof if you throw in the..."

Ask the seller to include extras in your offer. Ask for your closing costs to be paid for by the seller. Ask for a home warranty to cover electrical, plumbing, and appliances. This low cost insurance helped us with our well problems. A home warranty will give you peace of mind. If the seller won't pay for this, increase the sales price to cover it. A usual home warranty costs about $350 with add-ons for extra coverage such as wells, septic systems, and air-conditioning systems.

Once you feel that you've reached the seller's breaking point, offer something back to the seller. Allow extra time in moving out, help with moving, or extra assistance cleaning up. Think of the seller's problem and propose another solution reinforcing your kindness. Chitchat for awhile and then say, "Let's finish this up..." Fill in more blanks on your contract. Assume the seller is providing a title insurance policy and paying closing costs. Sellers can always say no and cross out anything you write down.

Give the seller a short time to make a decision. Sometimes a short response time is beneficial to you. The more time you give the seller to accept or counter your offer, the more offers may come in. Putting pressure on the seller for a quick response can get you a better deal.

Extras like the stove, refrigerator, washer, dryer, and even some furnishings included in the sale make your upcoming transformation easier. Sell unattractive appliances later and replace them if needed. Meanwhile, it's convenient to use them during your work phase.

The time you make much of your money is when you purchase the property. Of course you won't get the money until later. You want instant equity, so buy right. Also, instant equity provides the opportunity to add on a second mortgage right away and get your purchase money plus more back.

How Investors Buy Houses for Half Price

Replicate many investors' techniques. Drive down any street, look for the messiest yard, take down the address, order a property profile from a title company, and then write a letter to the owner or send your postcard. To order a property profile, call any title insurance company, and ask for customer service. Ask for a property profile including comps faxed to you or mailed to your address. You do not need the 30 or 40 page complete property profile.

This system, based on California's custom, works differently in other states. Seek advice from another investor in your local area for your best method of finding owner's information. Going to the county recorder's office and perusing title records takes more time and effort.

The information you need is the owner's name and address and comparable sales in the area. The owner may not have the same address as the property. Occasionally, the property profile lists the owner's phone number. Contact the owner, stating your interest in the house, either by phone or mail. Hand-written letters and envelopes usually don't get thrown out as junk mail. Even if the owner has received investor's offers previously, you never can tell when the owner is ready to bargain.

Realtor Mike only buys houses that he can pick up for half the market price. You don't need to be so firm to make a nice profit. Depending on the condition of the property and your intentions—keeping for a rental or flipping—calculate your estimated profit potential and then determine what dollar amount works for you. Will you be happy with a $20,000 profit or does it take more for you to get involved?

Tips on Buying and Closing

Don't get emotionally involved with one property. You have no time for disappointment and do not want pressure to pay too much for the property. Don't wait for the perfect property. Make lots of offers. This is the only way to get a good deal.

Don't get discouraged if it seems hard to find a bargain house. It sometimes takes us weeks to find a house. We are happy with three or four a year to make $90,000 to $120,000. One of our selling agents said we could make more profits by buying more houses and making less on each property. He wanted to sell us one house a month for a profit of $15,000-20,000 each. We just don't want to work that much and prefer to make more on each project.

Strong Deposits Grab Seller's Attention, But...
Offers with large earnest money deposits,

considered stronger than a low, weaker deposit, have a better chance of acceptance. HUD requires a $2,000 deposit. Generally, we give a deposit of only $1,000 when making an offer. Some real estate agents push for a large deposit. Tell them to increase the deposit if needed, after the home inspection report.

Be careful with your deposit checks. We once gave a real estate agent a check with an offer and she deposited it into her in-house escrow company. We did not get the property and it took over a week to get the funds back from the escrow company, and then our bank put a hold on the escrow company check!

Accepted Offers

Congratulations on finding your first doghouse! Ask your lender for a good-faith estimate with a rate lock and sufficient time to close. Get a signed copy. Check this against the final statement before closing to make sure the broker isn't double charging you. Loan brokers get paid by the lenders who underwrite the mortgage as well as by the borrowers.

Escrow or Closing

If possible, use your pre-selected escrow officer, but the seller may insist on his own escrow company. Usually, the listing agent influences the seller's choice. Don't let real estate agents force you into using an in-house escrow company owned by their broker. Some in-house escrows are fast and efficient, but others delay the process because they are too busy or inefficient. If the

selling agent insists on a broker-owned escrow,
ask for a reduction in your deposit because you
don't want to tie up your money when you aren't
sure of their competence. Also, ask for a fee
reduction for your escrow if they cause any delays
by being too busy.

Important Warning!
You can't afford to lose your rate lock or loan
costs locked in the good faith estimate. Even
though the interest rate isn't all that important
for resale properties, your loan costs are. Once,
because our good faith estimate expired, we were
forced to pay exorbitant fees to save a deal.

Ask your escrow officer for a copy of their escrow
checklist and follow the progress. Keep everyone
on track to ensure closing of your doghouse.
Realtors, lenders, and escrow officers are
dreadfully busy. Your regular contact keeps the
momentum moving forward. Follow the progress
of the appraisal, the termite inspection, home
inspection, and loan commitment from your
lender. You need everything in place in a timely
manner so you can sign loan documents and
close when you want, not whenever it happens.

Sometimes a longer escrow benefits you. The
property should go up in value and you aren't
paying for it yet. However, the sooner you close
escrow, the sooner you can make your
transformation and make your profit.

Funding Conditions

When everything appears to be submitted, call your lender. Put pressure on her or him to find out what conditions, if any, need satisfying for funding. Last minute delays cost you, especially when purchasing property from a government agency like HUD, which fines daily for each day over 45 days. This fine costs less than the usual monthly mortgage costs, so I don't get alarmed about it. Take note, though: too many delays void many purchase contracts.

Annoying last-minute conditions cause additional stress and scare sellers if they think the sale is faulty. Without careful monitoring, everything falls apart during this time. This is another reason I love a good lender with everything done in the beginning and a good real estate agent who knows how to handle the lender. Conditions that we have encountered include the latest bank statements and credit issues. Lenders run your credit again just before funding to check for undesirable changes. Usually credit issues discovered at the last minute cause problems with little time to fix them. The last-minute issue we dealt with on our last purchase was our son's new high-dollar mortgage appearing on my husband's credit report.

Taking Title

Some investors prefer to purchase properties in a corporation. This is one way to avoid liabilities and possibly taxes. Most real estate investors we know buy in their name, not a corporation's. They get an umbrella liability insurance policy for three million dollars, covering all of their real estate assets.

The easiest way to finance your investment property is to buy it the old fashioned way—in your own name. You can obtain personal financing much more easily than financing for a corporation. After you make a profit, get expert help setting up a corporation, if you wish. Married couples need to think about their financing capabilities and possibly take title in escrow in only one partner's name. After closing, the other partner's name may be added depending on state law. In California, we put our property into a limited trust to avoid probate court, just in case something happens to us.

Title Insurance

Before you make an offer, get a preliminary title report—"prelim"—from your real estate agent or from your title insurance company. You want to be sure you can get a "clear title." Properties in probate often take years to be transferable.

Normally, the seller provides title insurance for the buyer's protection and the buyer pays for a separate title insurance policy for the lender. If your seller only owned the property for a short time, you both may be able to save money by a reissue of the seller's original policy.

Ask your title insurance company if they have any policies about quick resales. You may be able to pay a little extra to cover a free title insurance policy for your later sale. Some title insurance

companies will sell you a binder in addition the
title insurance policy for about ten percent more
and you can transfer this to your prospective
buyer.

Buying Time
Now that you have found your doghouse and
secured a great purchase contract with financing
arranged, you are ready to enter the final escrow
phase or closing of your investment property.
Make use of this waiting time by planning in
detail your upcoming transformation.

Chapter Five

Planning During Escrow

While waiting for closing, spend time planning your work and materials needed to ensure a quick transformation process and save money. During this time, gather bargain supplies needed but keep your bank cash reserves at the level required for your mortgage to fund. Do not charge up your credit accounts.

During the purchase phase or escrow, get a jump start on your transformation and ask for an early walk-through. Your real estate agent usually schedules a walk-through about three days prior to closing. You need more time than this for planning.

First, get a loose-leaf notebook with pockets and paper. Tie a string to a pen and your workbook. Learn to keep this workbook with you—you never know when you will find something for which you need the dimensions. Keep a mileage record for tax purposes and a list of telephone numbers for easy contact. (These record forms and other helpful worksheets available in *Doghouse to Dollar$ Workbook* make this task easy.)

Create an escrow checklist and once a week contact your lender, escrow officer, real estate agents or sellers to make sure no problems arise. Keep appraisers, termite inspectors, home inspectors and other services on track. Try to meet these professionals at the property to cover your interests because you need the property to meet your lender's qualifications.

Arrange Fire Insurance

Shop around for a fire insurance policy as soon as you open escrow to avoid getting stuck at the end of escrow without your policy in place. Your auto or current homeowner's insurance company may offer a discount for adding another property. Get quotes for group insurance through your college, credit union, or business associations. Other discounts apply for those over age 55. Ask other real estate investors for fire insurance references. My carpet company owner, an active investor, gave me the best reference for an insurance agent who has saved me thousands of dollars on premiums.

Sometimes it's hard to get fire insurance for investment properties and many companies will not insure a vacant house at all. For this reason, and for many others, dress up your property to look inhabited. Insurance companies often send a reviewer out to photograph your property a few days after close of escrow.

Insurance Warning!

Our insurance company cancelled our homeowner's policy on our primary residence because of our dog. The insurance reviewer checking on the condition of the property took a photo of our kind old dog who loves everyone. Replacement insurance cost us hundreds more.

Just be aware of insurance company regulations. They avoid large dogs and vacant houses.

Take "before" photographs to help remember details and to inspire your ideas for the makeover. **Take notes** on existing conditions and changes required.

Measure Everything

Take a sturdy contractor's tape measure or a laser measure and measure all the rooms, including doors, windows, and details such as the width of the sink if it needs replacing.

Imagine Your Finished Product

Close your eyes and imagine your future dollhouse from a buyer's point of view. Where will you park and what do you see? How do you approach the front door? First impressions sell your dollhouse. If a qualified buyer knows the property meets price, bedroom, and bathroom requirements and loves the home from first sight—you have a sale.

The approach to your dollhouse is critical. Picture a welcoming pathway to the front door. Homes that make you walk up a crowded driveway are not harmonious. Winding pathways denote a relaxed attitude while more formal straight and wide walkways indicate grandeur.

Front doors painted in a bright color create cheerful thoughts. Essential, attractive address numbers and bright flowers underscore happy feelings. Let your imagination run freely while you visualize the desired outcome.

Give plenty of consideration to the planning of your transformation. Continue your daydream walk-through of the dollhouse and make lists of desired changes. Keep in mind the neighborhood. Don't overbuild for your area and also don't be too cheap in an upscale neighborhood. Your dollhouse should be the cleanest and most inviting, not the most expensive. Spend your money wisely on improvements that don't cost a large amount and yet add visual, psychological, or resale value. You may not need to install new windows but they should be sparkling clean.

Window Shop
While waiting for possession—the day you get to start work on your doghouse—window shop for your expected building materials. Make a list of materials needed and lists of costs so you can plan a budget. Don't charge up your credit cards. Your lender will run your credit again just before funding to make sure you haven't over-extended yourself.

Grow Your Plants
Start cuttings from your garden or from friends' gardens. If you purchase sale plants now, they benefit from a chance to grow bigger. We cultivate an acre of red apple ground cover, which easily transplants for an instant greening of waste land.

Bargain Shop
Go to estate, garage, and yard sales, and watch

newspaper free ads. Look for props—mirrors, paintings, light fixtures, plants—paint, and a sturdy round dining table. A round dining table for four is perfect for signing the sales contract later and the table will be indispensable while working on your doghouse. Simple plastic garden chairs withstand abuse and still provide a sturdy place to rest.

Collect Free Building Supplies
Tell all your family and friends you will happily accept their castaways. Generous friends have given us windows, doors, a Jacuzzi bathtub, sinks, toilets, pond pumps, mirrors, light fixtures, paint, tools, furnishings, and much more for free.

Start collecting tools. Take an inventory of what you have and what you need. Look for good quality tools and power equipment at yard sales. We found that a step ladder with wide rungs saves our backs and legs. If you stand too long on a narrow rung, it hurts hours later. You may not need a ladder if you find a tall step stool. You also need eye-protection glasses, paper masks, gloves, a fire extinguisher, and a first aid kit including eye wash.

Design Plan: Dollhouse for Dollars

Selling Season
Calculate approximately your working time and then add on extra days for unexpected delays. Estimate your selling season—the time of year you will market your dollhouse. This is important

to plan your color scheme. Use cool colors—blue, green, gray—to sell during spring and summer. Use warm colors—yellow, red, maroon—to sell during fall and winter.

Overall Design Plan

Develop a general design plan considering your selling season, your budget, and your target market. Your design plan really depends on supply and demand. How many houses are for sale in your area? How many houses sell each week? Is the market cold, warm, or hot? Is it a seller's market or a buyer's market? If you think it may be difficult to sell your dollhouse, then you need to do more in your transformation to make your home stand out. If your market moves fast, plan to do less.

Remember, the transformation is different for a keeper. This also depends on the local rental market. Fix-ups for rental property where few rentals exist call for a "blow 'n go" approach—a general clean up, minimal paint, and repairs. On the other hand, increasing rental income calls for a more complex design plan utilizing hardy materials and a more pleasing outcome to attract higher-paying tenants. The building materials selected for a rental differ from the materials for a "fix 'n sell." Rentals need long-lasting upgrades; dollhouses need less durable but attractive details that a homeowner cares for and maintains.

Visualize your upcoming sale to help you plan your transformation. Daydream about the finished home and let your imagination scamper freely without limits. This fun activity lets your creativity surface, taking you to the ideas that make a difference in the final outcome. This happy planning stage makes the upcoming work exciting and is the part of the investment business I enjoy most.

Project what a future advertisement might say. Predict your selling ad and visualize the forthcoming dollhouse.

"Sugar Plum Cabin"
4 Bedroom enchanted home for all seasons.
Near ski resorts. Jewel-box inside and out.
Zero down. $1,500 mo OAC Phone #

Write out a narrative of your vision, like the following, to help you make decisions on your decorating supplies and building materials.

"Sugar Plum Cabin"
Buyers park in the street and walk over newly installed flat rock walkway (free). Buyers see plum-painted dollhouse with crisp white gingerbread, delicate flowers, green mini periwinkle (vinca minor), huge trees (existing). Buyers step onto new Victorian-trimmed front porch, see silver-painted house numbers, exquisite light fixture, and stained glass window in front door. Buyers enter front door and another stained glass door opposite catches their eyes. Glowing pine paneling and refinished floors, a great rock fireplace, and sparkling windows welcome buyers. Buyers step into kitchen and see

antique stove, new flooring, and clean countertop...

Visit DoghousetoDollhouseforDollars.com to see photographs of the finished cabin.

You can see how a visualization narrative helps to plan the transformation and determine building materials needed. Keep in mind: a dollhouse with a focus delights those viewing your hard work. I always imagined what the Sugar Plum Fairy would desire in her cabin when making purchases for this dollhouse. We uncovered the "exquisite light fixture" at Habitat for Humanity's *ReStore* for $5.00.

Brian and I took stained glass classes and made the windows with professional help. Our daughter Katie dug up the flat rocks on the property and made a sun pattern walkway and a moon-shaped flower planter. We repainted the house numbers and moved them. I hung crystals in the windows to catch the sunlight and add magic.

Room-by-Room Work Plan
Create a list of work and materials needed for each room. Estimate the time you think it will take for each task. Make an overall list of materials, supplies, and tools needed. The more planning completed prior to escrow closing, the easier and faster the transformation.

Helpers
Plan for your outside help. You need to pay for help to do the things beyond your capabilities,

like a new roof. If you hire outside help for the work you can do, you speed up the conversion and save money on mortgage payments and utilities. On the other hand, in California, our experience proved that property values go up more than the monthly expenditures.

Decide what you want to do and delegate the work that you don't. Locate handymen or day laborers to help you with projects you know how to supervise. Use caution: we experienced bad happenings with cheaters, thieves, and devious workers. Ask around for recommendations for day help. Watch the neighborhood for other helpers and talk to the neighbors about their work. Find skilled workers with good reputations whose invaluable help speeds up the transformation and ensures quality workmanship. Check to see if your insurance covers these workers and protect your hard-earned money from a lawsuit.

Sometimes, hiring professional help is worth the extra expense. We found professional painters work faster and therefore cost less than day laborers. Tile installers, carpet layers, and electricians know their trades and do a better job than most day laborers. Also, contractors should have their own disability and liability insurance— ask for a copy with your contract. Get everything in writing—work to be completed, costs, lists of specific materials to be used, time for completion, and payment schedule.

Painters

Because I like to mix our own paint from "oops" paint to save hundreds of dollars and fashion a harmonious blend of colors, I get quotes from professional painters for a labor price without their company supplying the paint. Professional painters seem to charge less for their work than other tradesmen. If you need to paint the entire interior and exterior of your doghouse, hiring a painter to do the outside speeds up the process and may save you a mortgage payment.

Utilities

Just prior to the close of escrow, after handing over your closing funds and signing your loan documents, schedule the utilities connection. Many busy utility companies take longer than expected to come out. You need at least water and electricity at the very beginning. You may need a huge rubbish dumpster for a big transformation. Some utility companies offer forms for you to fill out as an investor, which allow you to move your service for fewer fees to your next property. Ask them for a "clean and show" turn on charge, which costs less than the normal fee.

Although you can get by without natural gas or propane, these services help in many ways. The gas service technician turns on the service, checks for leaks, and turns on the furnace, range, and hot water heater for you. You don't want to be miserably cold while working in your property and warm water for hand washing feels nice. Also, when you get ready to sell your property, the buyers expect to check these features.

Additionally, during cool or cold selling seasons, the furnace provides warmth to best present your dollhouse and sell for highest profit.

Be there when the water is turned on. Find the location of the shut-off valve. You need to know how to turn off the water quickly to prevent flooding if a water pipe breaks. The water utility company can usually turn on the service and leave the water off under the heavy concrete cover. Sometimes it is difficult to turn the valve and once we had trouble finding the right specialized tool to do this. Moreover, the water service person assists you if any problem arises.

Mail

Check your mail at your new property. Closing agents and escrow companies habitually send your settlement papers and refund check to your new address, even if you ask them to send it elsewhere. Look for home improvement coupons which help you save on makeover costs.

Safety

Check safety issues, then clean up all trash and debris. You will need smoke detectors for your selling escrow, so go ahead and install them. Change the locks if you purchased a repossessed home or if you're not sure about the previous owner's integrity.

Feng Shui practitioners believe in getting rid of negative energy in a newly purchased home. They particularly like to clean the doorknobs inside and out to get rid of the prior occupant's negative auras. It's a good idea to get rid of all scum and possible germs as well.

Tell your helpers you expect them to clean up after themselves. Don't allow trash to build up. Keep a safe environment for all and avoid potential hazards.

Planning Payoff
Considerable time spent planning during escrow speeds your transformation time, saves you money on lengthy renovations, and ensures you the best overall design plan to achieve your ultimate goal of making money.

After all your hard work of finding, financing, and purchasing your investment property, celebrate your possession day. Congratulate yourself on a job well done! Get ready for the real fun!

Chapter Six

Transformation Psychology

Your satisfying and lucrative real estate business depends upon your correct assessment of profit potential, successful purchasing, and triumphant transformation of a doghouse into a dollhouse. The renovation process includes the physical work and the choice of the best supplies to elicit maximum positive emotional effect. This chapter brings to light the psychological impact of design details which result in the desired transformation, promising the highest potential resale value. By incorporating the psychology of residential design, you intentionally choose how to transform your doghouse by using colors, textures, building materials, and decorations that assure your future speedy and cost-effective sale.

The psychology of residential design joins the entire home, inside and out. Using Design Psychology in your personal home is based on your own personal needs and preferences. Renovating a doghouse for dollars integrates generalized design ideas appealing to a broader spectrum of buyers.

Using Design Psychology to increase your real estate profits means that you learn how different decorating details and choices of materials affect human senses, and thereby emotions. Buyers view a prospective home with their eyes and yet their brain interprets what they see and feel according to subtle touches you purposefully use in your home makeover. Design details additionally influence our senses of touch, smell, hearing, and even taste.

Process of Transformation Psychology

Your real estate business is a step-by-step process. Your goal of composing a glorious home that buyers can't live without began with your planning of changes desired. Following our work process, from inception to realization, bit by bit, simplifies and organizes your makeover.

Photographs for Your Protection

Perhaps you took photographs during escrow with the seller's possessions filling the space. If your property was occupied during escrow, take "before" photographs again after closing for your own satisfaction and to show to future appraisers who ask why you expect to sell for so much more than your purchase price. Detailed photographs substantiate the property conditions compared to the final result. Avoid possible complications with your future sale by showing the appraiser all the improvements made to the property to get your deserved upgraded appraisal. This is crucial—the appraiser must give you credit for your work and expenses and not use your recent purchase price as market value.

Preview Open House Party

Invite your friends and family for a preview open house before you begin major work. Ask them to bring any unwanted household fixtures or

supplies, and ask them for any fix-up ideas, wild
or practical, that occur to them during their visit.
Record these ideas in a transformation journal
that you can refer to when you need fresh
inspiration.

Invitation

> Your presence is requested at Jeanette & Brian's
> Doghouse Open House.
> Come view our latest project and understand why we
> will be busy for the next month.
> Please bring cuttings from your garden and any
> unwanted paint.
> Any household or building material hand-me-downs
> will be greatly appreciated!
> Sunday afternoon, noon to four.

Once you finally get possession, your house may
seem overwhelming with all the work needed.
Plan a fun event to alleviate the weight of work
waiting for you.

Buying Materials for Drama

We usually spend about $12,000 for renovation,
including costs of materials and outside help.
Many investors spend much less, but I think they
make a great deal less too. We love taking a dirty
doghouse and turning it into a marvelous
showplace, and we're willing to invest more time
and money to achieve a dramatic transformation.

Every time you make a purchase for your
doghouse, record it and put the receipt in the
pocket of your workbook. Remember to keep

track of your mileage. Good record keeping saves you money on taxes.

Suppliers and Exquisite Details

You need to spend less to make more; yet, sometimes spending a little extra gives you greater profit. If you don't find what you want at a bargain price, go to an upscale retailer and look for sale items. Exquisite details can add dollars to your bank account faster. If you use ugly, cheap, or tacky fixtures, most likely you will sell for less profit, have a harder time selling, and make additional mortgage payments. Think about the difference between spending $100 more for a high quality fixture and paying an additional $1,500 mortgage payment.

We usually shop at **home improvement warehouses**. Discount stores also sell many useful household items. We buy lace curtains at Wal-Mart because they offer a better price than wholesale or making them ourselves.

Our favorite supplier is ReStore—the outlet for Habitat for Humanity. We bought light fixtures, window hardware, paint, switch-plate covers, house numbers, mirrors, sinks, and even beds for our cabin from ReStore. We signed up for ReStore's mailing list and they advise of upcoming half-price sales. ReStore also considers bargaining. The tagged price is not always the final price. I always ask for something free if I buy a lot at one time and I usually get it. Ask, "If I buy all this today, will you throw in that item?"

Another supplier is our own home. I upgraded our dishwasher and Brian installed the used one in a doghouse. We reuse window treatments, hardware, and much more as I either redecorate or improve our personal home.

Nursery License
We applied for a California nursery license to grow ground cover. This license also allows us to go to nursery trade shows and wholesale nurseries. This saves us money on plants, containers, and garden accessories.

Where to Start
Sometimes interior projects need attention prior to the exterior work to make your transformation possible. Getting the kitchen sink and a bathroom up and running takes priority. After this step, if weather permits, start outside.

First, the Roof
If the roof needs to be repaired or replaced, do this first to stop any further damage to the house. Also, roofers are messy and can injure your landscaping and new paint finish. However, sometimes roof a new roof is not in the fix-up budget. In this case, make the repairs later during your selling escrow and have the bill sent to escrow.

For functional roofs that look hideous, try paint. We painted the roof of our guesthouse. The roof, though discolored and unsightly, did not need to be replaced. We added water to the paint for a transparent finish.

Back of Guesthouse Before

Guesthouse After

Begin at the Street

After the roof decision, begin your transformation at the street. Befriend the neighbors and give them your phone number. They will watch the property for you and also may know someone who wants to buy your dollhouse. Also, get to know their dogs' names and make friends with them so dogs will not bark at you when you show the property in the future. Write down neighbor's and dog's names in your workbook.

Once you start fixing up your property, you inspire neighbors to work on their own front yard. All of our doghouse neighbors improved their front yards and some even painted their homes after we began the transformation process on our house. Upgrading the neighborhood helps raise the selling price of current homes on the market and increases your future sale price. By starting work outside, you give neighbors inspiration and time for them to work while you finish your project. This way, you benefit from their work as well.

Create an Exciting Exterior

Curb appeal is the most important challenge you face. Imagine your prospective buyers driving up and examining the property for the first time. Depending on the size of the home, you want them to exclaim "What a darling home!" or "Wow! Look at this mansion!" Buyers forgive little inadequacies in the property if they love the home from the first sighting.

Psychological Effects of Landscaping

Buyers *think* that they care about the inside of the house more than the landscaping. In reality, most buyers won't even get out of their car if the front landscaping lacks the promise of great details inside. The landscaping needs to arouse their hope and lure them with anticipation to view the entire home.

Plan for a lot of green and white in landscaping. Green conjures feelings of freshness and cleanliness; white flowers support the same feelings and show up better at night. Bright yellow flowers by the front door attract the buyer's eye from a distance (our eyes process yellow before any other color). Give forethought to the overall scents of flowering trees, bushes, vines, and flowers and take advantage of plants supporting the desired emotional outcome. You don't need to go overboard; plant enough to make an impression of healthy growth and detract from any barren spaces by creating focal points in the landscape.

Consider the existing flowering foliage and coordinate the colors. Think about your selling season and plan for flowering plants that perform well during that time. Also give thought to the desired atmosphere and use plants supporting this outcome. For instance, tropical, desert, forest, and beach environments differ in plant types. Choose plant types that harmonize within a theme.

Make a landscaping plan that results in your preferred emotional response. A wandering pathway to the front door psychologically feels better than a straight-shot walkway. Adding a water feature greatly enhances the ambiance. Moving water relaxes the body and mind and refreshes the spirit, enticing a buyer and increasing the value and marketability of your property. One dominating feature in the garden setting creates an unnatural, out-of-balance feeling. Balance a large fountain with another prominent piece like a pot similar in size and shape.

Start on the landscaping before working in the interior of the house to give plants time to grow. Plant the areas away from the house if you plan to paint the exterior. Include cuttings from your garden and your friends' gardens. I keep pots at home for propagating plants so I have them ready to go for our next doghouse transformation.

We transplanted cuttings of red apple all over this bank, which was full of dead weeds a couple of months earlier.

Sprinklers

Sprinklers systems need not cost much and they add value to the future sale. More important, sprinklers save you time watering while keeping your lawn healthy and green. If you can't water every day at your doghouse, install sprinklers with a timer. Save money by not adding a timer if you plan to consistently work at the site or check on your project regularly. Install your sprinkler system before you add landscaping or a new walkway. Home improvement warehouses have free seminars on how to install sprinkler and drip systems.

Emerald Lawns
Because of the water shortage in Southern
California, we use as little sod as possible. We
make the planted areas surrounding the lawn
larger and use lots of red apple ground cover. Red
apple is deep green, drought tolerant, grows
quickly, and for us—free! Most buyers still expect
a lawn, which replaces bleak settings with a
beautiful green richness. We purchase sod from a
local sod farm and get our sons to help schlep.

Majestic Trees
If you already have a statement tree at your
doghouse—great! Otherwise, if you need an
accent tree to add height to the setting or to
disguise a bad view, look for a great deal on as big
of a tree as you can handle, both budget wise and
physically. We hate digging large holes, so we
prefer overgrown five-gallon trees. Tall bushes or
trees planted in line with the corner of the house
soften the hard architectural edge and ground the
house with the earth.

Look for one-gallon shrubs or bushes that you
know grow quickly in your area. Also, many five-
inch perennials grow up or spread nicely in three
months. Think of the number three when
planning your garden—three of each plant
grouped together brings a professional touch and
a feeling of completeness to the landscaping.
Groups of six and nine of the same plant present
an expanse and make the area appear larger.

Fragrant Flowers
Think about the scents flowers exude into your

garden setting and plan for the eventual selling season. Wait to plant annuals until you are in the last phase of your transformation. Some exceptions to this, like sweet alyssum, spread and live until you're ready to sell. To economize, start flats of flower seeds for transplanting later.

Decorative bark, the finishing touch for a professional looking garden, helps prevent weeds and retains water. Save money on mulch or decorative bark by having a truckload delivered instead of buying it by the bag. We asked a tree company clearing around power lines to dump their waste in our back yard and received a lot of free mulch.

Side Yards and Sales Potential
The areas on the side of your dollhouse make little appreciable difference to your sale. Just make sure they are weed-free and clean. On the other hand, creating a beautiful view for a room looking out onto the side yard does double duty: window coverings are not necessary and the alluring garden setting attracts attention.

Backyards and Reality
We rarely get around to the back yards of our dollhouses. Buyers usually love a house before they get to the backyard. There is just so much else you can do and still make a great profit without working on the backyard. We usually leave something for the new homeowners to do.

We have improved various backyards by adding small porches, decks, and a few overgrown one-gallon privets. We use our garden props, a free standing gazebo and a wrought iron folding screen, which we move from house to house. We place large plants in containers, which we move and reuse, to add healthy growth to the atmosphere without a lot of work or expense.

Motivating Front Elevations

Examine the visual appeal of your front elevation, the house, garage, and structural amenities. More than just curb appeal—many details hidden from street view influence the overall impression. Consider the effect of the garage and parking areas. Dollhouses look better if the garage isn't overwhelming when you look at the home from the street. If the garage door visually stands out more than the front elevation, break up the huge door expanse with molding or paint it the same color as the siding.

An enticing entry landing makes buyers want to get out of their car. If you only have a little step, enlarge this area to make the entry appealing and significant. Create a front porch or spectacular patio entry and make it friendly, bright, and tempting. Add an attractive doormat to keep your dollhouse clean inside.

Check out the photographs of Orange Tree Cottage on the cover: Brian added the front porch, shutters, and flower box to create a welcoming and charming feel on an otherwise bland house. We purchased the new light fixture at ReStore. Hummingbirds gathering around the feeder and the chair "props" suggest a relaxed and happy home.

Garages and the Psychology of Parking

Avoid blocking the view from inside the home with vehicles. Designate parking areas with rock borders or any type of edging material.

We never spend much time working on a garage interior—just working in it. The garage interior makes little difference to most buyers. Just clean and neat is all right; you don't need to paint the interior. Garage floor cleaners, similar to cat litter, work well for grease spots.

Exterior Electrical

Replace existing electrical fixtures with advice from your local home improvement center. Lowe's and Home Depot offer free classes on electrical projects. A shiny new brass entry lantern greatly enhances an entry landing.

Water features like ponds or a water fountain significantly add to the setting. Think about safety with ponds—the front yard needs appropriate fencing. We love creating Koi ponds at our main homes. For upscale neighborhoods, a Koi pond makes a nice addition. For most fixers, a small water fountain near the entry noticeably magnifies the desired feelings of luxury and tranquility.

Gingerbread

Extra amenities that help sell our dollhouses quickly for more than the asking price include window boxes, decorative gingerbread, fancy porch railings, front door surrounds, and shutters. Look at Sugar Plum Cabin Front Porch on page 27: Brian built the front porch, in the style of our Florida Victorian porches, and added gingerbread under the eaves.

Sugar Plum Cabin Doors

Fancy Front Doors

Study your home from the street and make sure the front door and entry area stands out and outshines the garage door. Front doors should be painted a shiny-gloss cheerful color unless they show off beautiful wood. Add decorative molding to a plain door. Replace unattractive front doors and adorn with new locksets to appreciably heighten appeal. We scavenged ReStore to unearth great egg-shaped locksets for a low price. I love the way this shape feels in my hand.

Painting Front Doors

Choose a happy color like red, green, or yellow-tan. For entry doors in a recess or shadows, pick a lighter shade. Consider the exterior colors and venture out for a new complementary color. Paint the front door a separate joyful color.

At Elise and Dan's house, we painted a metal security door with brownish-red gloss paint. Then Brian applied copper patina paint with a big paintbrush as I dabbed the paint off with plastic bags. The existing dirty front door turned out so spectacular, even the appraiser remarked on its appeal (and most appraisers typically don't say much). I believe the front door and the entry wall-fountain sold the home, which sold for more than any other house had previously sold for on the street.

Choosing Exterior Paint Colors for Profit

Paint makes a huge difference. It cleans up the mess and quickly adds the most value for the least expense. Choose a light color that goes with the roof unless you live in snow country—light colored houses hurt the eyes when surrounded by snow. Lighter colors on the siding make a house look bigger. Choose colors that enhance existing brick or stone facing. For properties with too many types of brick and stone creating a jumbled appearance, paint over one to blend it with the siding. For stucco siding that looks good without defects, just clean or pressure wash the house, and then paint the trim.

Think fun colors for a fast sale. Go to the extra trouble for a third or forth color on the exterior. This adds definition to details. Use gloss or semi-gloss paint on wood trim. You don't have to go to all the trouble of the "Painted Ladies" in Savannah or San Francisco. However, using more than two colors makes your house stand out from the other homes for sale and gives buyers a reason to fall in love.

Psychology of Exterior Paint Colors

Take into account the ultimate sales price of your remodeled home. Certain colors, especially muted, complex shades, attract wealthy or highly-educated buyers, whereas buyers with less income or less education generally prefer simple colors. A *complex color* contains tints of gray or brown. A *simple color* is straightforward and pure. Complex colors usually require more than one word to describe, like sage green compared to green.

Think about your selling season and your climate when choosing paint colors. This relates to your overall design plan too. Try to envision your final product, such as a cooling desert oasis or warm, inviting haven.

Usually we paint the exterior of our dollhouses in light colors because they appear larger. However, our cabin in the woods looks richer painted a dark color. I considered the usual cabin colors of dark brown and barn red, but fell in love with Olympic's "Gooseberry" paint.

Paint stores give out many brochures with combinations of exterior paint colors. Notice how most combinations include three colors. Limiting your paint selection to only two colors limits your income potential. Combinations of colors that excite you make your job more fun and attract buyers too.

Check out the colors of neighboring houses and pick out colors which harmonize yet stand out from the crowd. Clashing colors detract from the overall setting of the neighborhood. I am grateful that the houses on either side of Sugar Plum Cabin are wood shake and beige instead of yellow and red.

Mixing Your Own Paint for Savings and Harmony

Purchase bargain unwanted paints at home improvement and paint stores to save hundreds of dollars on your transformation expenses. Invest in a paint mixer attachment for your electric drill. These low-cost tools work so much better than a free paint stick! I recommend you use only water-based paints. Technology improvements in latex and acrylic paints make painting easier than old fashioned oil-based paints and provide a great finish.

By mixing your own paints, you guarantee a harmonious result for the entire home. The paint colors blend nicely from the exterior to the interior and from room to room. For instance, for

Orange Tree Cottage we purchased ten assorted gallons of paint from ReStore. These paints, donated by Lowe's, were returned by the original buyers, perhaps because the color wasn't what they expected. We used a fifteen-gallon plastic kitchen trash can for mixing the paint and then poured the paint back into the empty cans. This mix included a lot of blues, greens, and grays. The color ended up a complex sage-green, which complemented the existing teal-green tile floor.

We used our trash-can paint outside first, and then added white interior paint to continue the same colorway inside. We first painted the living room and a bathroom. Then I added a little green to the paint and painted a bedroom. For each room we added a little more semi-gloss white from a five-gallon purchased for trim and the kitchen walls. We saved a glass jar full of each custom paint blend for each room for touch up.

Paint experts tell me to only mix the same type of paints: exterior latex with exterior latex; interior acrylic with interior acrylic; interior latex with interior latex. However, we have successfully mix exterior paints with interior paints. You need plenty of ventilation when using exterior paints inside. The amount of sheen makes little difference in mixing paints, unless you want a particular finish. Satin or eggshell paint finish reflects desirable light. Flat finishes best disguise wall imperfections.

At Sugar Plum Cabin, I started with five gallons of rejected baby-blue paint as the base. I added a quart of black paint to gray down the baby-blue. As we progressed through each bedroom, I added white semi-gloss latex paint to the mix.

At Elise's and Dan's dollhouse, I added amber pigment to five gallons of boring beige "oops" paint. You can pick up paint tint at most paint suppliers. Add paint tint slowly because a little goes a long way. We started in the main bedroom with the darker color and added white as we went along. The lightest shade ended up in the living room with the 23-foot-high ceiling. To balance the house colors, we painted the bathrooms a light teal. The mosaic glass tiles Elise used for the entry water fountain and bathroom counter were amber, teal, blue, and green.

Makeover the Interior for Maximum Profit

Once you finish improving the exterior, it's time to start on the interior. Details using psychology to increase real estate profits for specific rooms follow general techniques applicable to the entire interior.

Decorative Paint

Stencils and decorative paint give more depth to a room and make buyers remember your home.

Photo by Dawn Burk, Interior of Sunny Point
Stencil and decorative paint by Jeanette Fisher

Paint Preparation

Proper preparation is an unenjoyable but necessary step before painting. TSP and hot water work well to cut greasy fingerprints and TSP leaves no residue requiring rinsing. For bad stains, prime with Kilz water-based stain blocker. Invest in a good canvas drop cloth; plastic shifts and spreads drips instead of absorbing them. Workers walk across the plastic, pick up paint on their shoes, and track it everywhere. Even if you plan to replace all the flooring, you want to avoid paint tracks outside on the sidewalks or in your car.

To remove wallpaper, use liquid fabric softener and hot water instead of wallpaper remover. Get a "Paper Tiger," available at paint centers, to score the paper. For stubborn wallpaper, rent a steamer. This is not my favorite job—we stripped painted-over wallpaper forever in our Victorian home. In another fixer, I discovered glazing over brightly-colored wallpaper tones down hot colors. Today, I avoid wallpaper stripping altogether, but I still clean toilets.

Patching

Holes in the wall? Use joint compound with a taping knife to fill holes. When dry, either sand the rough areas or wash with a wet sponge. Patch large holes with a piece of sheetrock and tape before the joint compound dries. Sometimes, you need to go over a patch a second time. Use flat paint to mask uneven patching and walls. A glossy finish highlights blemishes more. Decorative finishes, such as color washing and sponge painting, also effectively obscure imperfections in uneven walls.

When you paint with a roller, use an extension pole and make wide sweeps up and down. Stand back from the wall to get as big of an area with one stroke as possible. This painter's technique is the fastest way other than spraying, which makes a huge mess. Besides, masking-off for a paint sprayer takes too much time. We use a sprayer along with a large cardboard shield mostly outside to paint large expanses of siding quickly. Sprayers use considerably more paint to cover the same area. You can rent paint sprayers but be aware—it takes practice to paint with a sprayer. You can easily end up with overspray everywhere, runs difficult to remove, and you may use up all your paint before you are done.

Painters usually paint the ceiling, then the walls, and finally the trimwork. I like to paint the glossy surfaces first so that I save time and effort by avoiding masking off. Flat and satin paint finishes effortlessly wipe off the glossier trim paint. Usually I do the painting with help from my children and my husband does all the other harder work.

The highest-quality cutting brush is a worthwhile investment. With practice, you learn to cut-in paint next to another color without masking and save time. I keep a wet rag handy to wipe off mistakes as I paint. Keep the brush end wet to the point where it almost drips for a smooth finish. With practice, a good quality trim paint, and a superb brush, you can paint trim with only one coat. Buying good quality trim paint and brushes saves time and thereby saves money.

Instead of wasting paint, water and my time, I put my paint-covered rollers and brushes in plastic grocery bags when I take a break. When I'm finished for the day, I place the bags in my freezer. The frozen paint tools thaw out incredibly fast—even after months.

Keep a Little Paint
After you finish a room and before you add
another color of paint to your base paint, pour off
a glass jar full of paint. Label the paint according
to the room and keep it for touch ups. The carpet
installers usually mar your paint finish a little
and you too may scrape it accidentally. Also,
when you look at the room later under different
lighting, areas needing touchup mysteriously
appear.

Lighting Psychology

Lighting: the most important factor
of Residential Design Psychology

Natural daylight makes buyers feel happy. As a
mood elevator, daylight brings feelings of comfort.
In contrast, dark and closed-in rooms depress us.
Keep windows clear unless a dreadful view
detracts from the setting. In this case, use light-
filtering fabric just heavy enough to obscure the
undesired view. Plan your other window coverings
to open during the day and to close at night.
Black holes at night make some people feel
uncomfortable.

Buyers respond better to homes brightly
illuminated, and sufficient lighting helps make
rooms look bigger. Brighten dark corners with
uplights set behind houseplants. Augment
daylight with white halogen light bulbs that best

imitate sunlight. If you want to save money, replace these bulbs with less-costly bulbs during escrow to reuse on your next venture.

Plan lighting for your selling season. Cool-white lighting provides the emotional effect best for spring and summer. Warm pink and amber colored bulbs best achieve the desired emotional support for fall and winter. Remember that shades and globes influence the color emanated from a fixture.

Interior Electrical

Learn how to be an electrical wizard by attending free classes at your local home improvement center. Make sure you shut the electricity off at the main source before touching wires.

Brian replaced all the chipped and painted-over electrical plugs at Orange Tree Cottage. He then added new switch plate covers. This low-cost improvement really helped clean up the place. It was amazing how this small detail made the house look brand new.

New Light Fixtures
Stunning new lighting fixtures significantly improve the ambiance of a home. Replace unsightly or nonworking light fixtures to greatly enhance the sales potential. Look for bargain lighting fixtures on sale in lighting stores, home improvement centers, at ReStore, and at yard sales. Our local contractor lighting showroom sells discontinued and deeply discounted light fixtures to the public.

It is possible to reuse many fixtures that come with your property, especially dining room chandeliers. If the dining light fixture is too small or unimpressive, re-hang it in the entryway, bathroom, or a bedroom. Dress up plain chandeliers by adding inexpensive decorative shades. The best source I've found for these shades is Wal-Mart. I like to spray paint the interior of shades with gold paint to intensify the glowing mood.

At Sugar Plum Cabin, we found a yard sale chandelier, used Wal-Mart shades we trimmed with gold braid, and added crystal drops packaged as Christmas ornaments purchased from a mail order catalog. The final light fixture cost only about $35.00 but dazzles like a top-notch chandelier.

Sugar Plum Dining Room with dressed-up chandelier and custom built-in pantry.

Flooring & Feelings

Buyers *think* they love Italian tile and other hard floor surfaces. However, they *feel* happier walking on softer surfaces such as padded carpeting and laminate. Balance hard and soft surfaces, considering the selling season secondarily. Long-term decorating items like floor coverings become the backdrop all year long. Add temporary warmth and texture with area rugs or coolness and texture with sisal and seagrass mats.

Flooring Colors for Selling

Choose neutral, light colors for floor surfaces that won't clash with the new homeowner's furnishings. Buyers realize they can easily paint over colored walls, whereas changing floor surfaces is difficult and costly. The color you bring into play for selling and staging your home is best left to other areas than the flooring.

Hard Floor Surfaces

Use appropriate flooring surfaces aimed at your target market. Tile floors in bathrooms, considered an upgrade, increase property value and sales appeal. Learning to install tile floors saves you in costs, not time. Many types of vinyl effectively imitate more expensive surfaces and your cash outlay for professional installation is unexpectedly little.

Install the kitchen flooring before the appliances. Usually, you save money by hiring the same installers to put in the hard flooring at the same time as the carpeting. However, this is a balancing act. You want to finish painting and any construction prior to carpet installation.

Using carpeting instead of hard flooring in bathrooms saves even more money and ties the spaces together for a more spacious feeling. This works better in a main bedroom suite or a property aimed for adults only.

Carpeting

Before making the decision to replace wall-to-wall carpeting because of stains, try cleaning it first. I tested my carpet company owner's trick on Sugar Plum Cabin's spotted carpeting in the bedrooms. Following her advice, I sprayed Windex directly on the spots, scrubbed lightly with a scrub brush, and wiped up the spots with a wet rag. The spots disappeared! Lighter fluid also removes difficult stains, including some paints.

Buyers love new carpeting, especially if they get the chance to select it themselves. If the existing carpeting is truly awful, rip it out and clean the floors. What does the home look like? Sometimes, investors offer the home for sale at this point and offer a carpeting allowance. Because the property shows much better completed with all flooring in place, we go ahead and install it.

Look for a carpet wholesaler or warehouse specializing in discontinued carpeting and roll ends. Rummage around for a roll end or large discontinued piece with sufficient amounts for an entire small house. Or, do what we did at Elise and Dan's: use three carpet roll ends of the same line for different areas of your dollhouse.

If you need financing for your carpet, large carpet chain stores as well as home improvement centers offer easy-payment plans for homeowners. Search for a payment option with no payments for a time period exceeding your transformation and sale time period.

Payback of Window Treatments

Because you plan to show the property mainly during daylight hours, think about your selling season, market conditions, and the benefits of window treatments. Fabric-free walls visually cool the room during summer days unless the hot sun streams in. In that case, light-filtering cool white fabric brings cooling shade. In cooler seasons, more substantial window coverings supplement a positive emotional impact with warmth, texture, and color. Fabrics soften hard wall surfaces while increasing visual warmth on cold days.

Real estate market conditions influence decisions regarding window treatments. Hot markets require fewer embellishments to sell, whereas increased competition with many listings similar to yours require extras like window coverings to attract buyers. Buyers appreciate the privacy provided by window coverings, so if a neighboring house seems intrusive, add light-filtering window coverings.

Window coverings and hardware bring architectural interest to a plain room and block unattractive views. A simple treatment with lengths of gossamer fabric add visual texture to monotonous walls or an empty room. Besides adding texture in the design, fabric colors supplement your desired emotional impression.

In Sugar Plum Cabin, we spray-painted a PVC pipe and ReStore hardware with gold leaf, covered unattractive but functional existing mini-blinds with lace curtains from Wal-Mart, and hung an antique mirror to dress up the main bedroom.

Beautiful corbels and window hardware add design details to bare, unfurnished rooms. I use painted wood closet rods, heavy gauge PVC (sold for plumbing), copper pipe, and bamboo instead of expensive, thinner curtain rods. These little extras dress up an otherwise simple box-like space.

Fireplaces & Focal Points

Check out the fireplace. If necessary, hire a chimney sweep, especially if plan to sell during the fall or winter months. Don't wait until you're showing your property to discover billowing black smoke filling your dollhouse with dirty soot. A hospitable fire not only increases the physical warmth, it adds moving light, which people respond to positively on a subtle, primal level.

Fill unused fireplaces with a plant or candelabra. An empty black hole doesn't add cheer to the setting. In summer, refreshing scented candles in the fireplace furnish the much-loved moving light, generating little heat and augmenting the buyer's sense of smell.

In main rooms without a fireplace, impressive views, or architectural features, create interest with a prominent accessory or furnishing as a focal point. Rooms with a focal point remain in your prospective buyers' minds so they choose your dollhouse instead of another property. Avoid dull rooms with a closed-in boxy feeling by using your imagination and props that entice buyers.

Props and Profits

Visit nearby model homes and examine the way the decorators furnished the homes. Notice how the homes are under-furnished—just enough accessories to make a superb presentation but not too much to make a space seem crowded or small. Using a few props to dress up your dollhouse helps you sell for the maximum profit in several ways:

- Props chosen with underlying psychological benefit supplement the emotional reactions desired, including the perceived room temperature.
- Props add perspective with visual depth—vacant rooms look flat.
- Props help to keep property in the mind of buyers who view many houses.
- Props are focal points for buyers to imagine their own furnishings in the home and get them to think about living in the space.

Simple props define a space and setting. Yard sale finds, tree branches, and a velvet lap throw from Target make a corner interesting and cozy.

Embellishments Equal Extra Dollars

Accessories which we use over and over to dress up different properties include: potted plants, paintings, mirrors, lightweight round tables with exquisite fabric skirts, and antique side chairs. We have an uncomfortable but great-looking antique sofa, upholstered in leopard print, which we move from dollhouse to dollhouse for visual appeal.

A sturdy table and chairs to sign contacts is invaluable to you. Don't let motivated buyers get away because it is too difficult to finalize the sale at the property. A simple card table with a striking fabric skirt adds soft texture to rooms with few furnishings. This helps counter the bleak emotional impact of hard surfaces and vacant spaces.

Borrow props from your own home. This saves money and time spent shopping. Also, when you bring the item home again, it seems to show up more and have more importance. Since you will spend most of your free time investing in your future by working on your doghouse, you shouldn't worry about missing a few accessories from home.

Plan your interior plants and flowers for your selling season. Pick up vases and containers at yard sales. Take advantage of what you have growing either at your dollhouse, at home, or from friends. Freshly cut green tree branches add visual coolness in warm weather and autumn leaves add visual warmth in cool weather.

Psychology of Mirrors

Take advantage of a tried and true sales technique: World Book Encyclopedia sales people asked the prospective buyer where they would put their bookcase filled with the Encyclopedia.

Once the buyers visualized the set in their home, they were ready to sign the contract. Mirrors bring subtle psychological value to your dollhouse. *The buyers see themselves in the property.*

Orange Tree Cottage: Mirror from bathroom, roses from the garden, dollar candle sconces

It is generally easy to find mirrors at yard sales. We have many mirrors purchased for $2.00 to $25.00 that we use again and again. Sometimes you can reuse mirrors that come with your doghouse. We took down a discolored mirror in the bathroom at Orange Tree Cottage; I took five minutes to "antique" the wood frame with a wash of white paint and hung the mirror over the mantle. The buyers requested this mirror and candle sconces as part of the sale!

Paintings and Proceeds

Add visual depth to the space with landscape paintings that present a great distance. Paintings also disguise the fact that your dollhouse doesn't have any real architectural features like a fireplace or crown moldings. Choose paintings that augment your color scheme and the emotions you want to evoke, like a cool mountain spring or warm desert.

Props and Financial Returns

Don't use family heirlooms because buyers often see something they just have to have with the sale. To sweeten the sale, we agreed to the buyer's request for a large new mirror at Elise and Dan's dollhouse. Purchased at Costco for the entry space, this mirror enlarged the space, brightened the dark corner, and reflected the new stained glass window, effectively doubling the window's prominence. Too bad the buyers didn't ask for the $2.00 mirror instead. This instance demonstrates the benefit of spending a little more for a higher profit. We sold this house for more than any house had previously sold for on the street. And, we saved a great deal of money on economical paint, light fixtures, and carpeting. The grand mirror was worth the extra expense.

Don't go overboard with props. You don't want to overcrowd the space or even come close to furnishing it. Buyers like to visualize their own furnishings in your dollhouse.

Buyers like clean unblemished walls. Examine your dollhouse with the imaginary eyes of a buyer. You don't want to mar up the new paint finish by hanging accessories on all the walls. However, mirrors and landscape paintings with distant horizons visually expand the space. Carefully consider the trade off, a small hole in the wall for an improved presentation. Easily paint over the small holes with your saved paint at close of escrow.

Individual Spaces and Rooms

You have 15 seconds to sell your dollhouse!

Enticing Entrances

When entering a potential home, most buyers know within *fifteen seconds* if they like the house or not. Rest outside your closed front door for a minute and clear your thoughts. Open the door from a perspective buyer's viewpoint. What immediately catches your eye? A long expansive view all the way out to the back fence or a wall that blocks vision? Play up the first area seen when entering the home. Create an exciting entrance and strategically place a mirror to capture your buyer's image in the space.

Inviting Living and Family Rooms

To make the most of your property, the living and family rooms need to seem large. Decorative paint finishes add visual depth to small rooms. Use mostly light colors for carpeting, ceilings, and walls.

Most investors paint everything inside white. I have much more success using color on the walls. Using your creativity is part of the fun in transforming a doghouse into a dollhouse. Additionally, stark white walls bring cold, harsh feelings into unfurnished houses. Compare the feelings generated by all white walls and off-white carpeting to feelings generated by warm colors and exciting carpeting. Notice the way model home decorators include color and paint over basic white walls.

Create Architectural Interest

If the room does not have a fireplace, a view, or any architectural features, adorn with details such as crown moldings, window dressings, or bookcases. Think creatively, not expensively. If you found a desirable neighborhood and created an exceptionally clean house, this may be enough. Yet, adding little details makes your dollhouse stand out and furthers your goal of selling quickly for more money.

Add Visual Depth

Notice the depth added by the painting and how a few
accessories doll up Sugar Plum Cabin.

Mirrors and paintings not only increase the visual
depth of the space, they bring into play wanted
emotional support. If you don't choose to add any
furniture at all, don't go overboard with wall
hangings because they will look out of place. A
mirror or landscape painting works nicely over a
fireplace, a bookcase, or a simple shelf.

Dynamic Dining Areas

A true dining room is a luxury in many areas and
you can play up this room with exquisite wall
treatments or window coverings. Dress up your
round table with a pretty tablecloth and a vase of
flowers or green cuttings from your garden.

Because dining rooms get little use, painting with dramatic colors heightens the uniqueness of the amenity.

Orange Tree Cottage dining area

At Orange Tree Cottage, we created a dining area out of a back porch, used a metal garden table covered with a white tablecloth, and borrowed antique chairs from our home. I purchased organza curtains and a gorgeous chandelier from Penney's on sale with an additional 25% off coupon and hung a lovely garage sale painting (reused in room pictured on page 136). The resulting dining room provided homey, welcoming feelings to the vacant house.

Merry Kitchens

The kitchen, typically the most important room for you to spend money on, needs to feel bright, spacious, and merry. Consider your ultimate fantasy kitchen in your target market price range. Granite, limestone, and marble indicate luxury homes, whereas laminate indicates economy. Many laminate countertops copy the more expensive surfaces and look truly attractive.

You may not need granite countertops, but unbroken tile is a must. Tile countertops cost less than most other surfaces if you install them yourself. Seek advice from local independent tile shops that often sell for less than home improvement discount stores and have more time to help you. Paint over unattractive Formica or laminate countertops with deck paint for a fast cleanup and savings.

We found that Restore4 really works well to get rust and other stains out of sinks and faucets. The kitchen sink has to be super clean, or you must replace it. A good faucet is essential. Most prospective buyers turn on the faucet to check its water pressure.

Paint the kitchen walls a light color, such as pale yellow or pale green semi-gloss. Kitchens painted in food colors *feel* right. Painting wood trim bright white with gloss paint adds instant cleanliness and light reflection.

Valley View Kitchen: Katie painted the ceiling above the sink red, which casts a pink glow on the white and provides enticing visual interest. The unusual placement of a stencil on the floor makes the kitchen outstanding rather than ordinary.

Consider the cabinet finish—white cabinets look better against a colored backdrop. Wood cabinets can be cleaned up with TSP if greasy and touched up with Orange Glo. If the cabinets are distressed, you can enhance this popular look by sponging white paint over them or just paint all white with gloss paint for a fresh and clean appearance. We rarely paint the interior of the cabinets—just remove unsightly shelf paper and clean well.

Lengths of counter space with no appliances make the area appear larger. Just a few props in the kitchen make a plain space feel like home. Sometimes, just hanging a pretty colorful hand towel gives just enough punch to enliven the kitchen. We use vases of roses cut from the garden or pots of greenery instead of kitchen accessories to bring about the desired psychological impact.

Mirrors in the Kitchen?
Follow Feng Shui masters and hang mirrors above stoves placed against a wall so that the cook sees who is behind him. Placing a mirror above a sink with no window provides the same secure feeling plus reflects light, reflects the buyer's image in the kitchen, and adds visual space.

Appropriate Appliances

Buyers look for good kitchen appliances, and new appliances greatly increase the sales potential. Compare your home to others in your area. If a dishwasher is the norm, your dollhouse should have one. Many lenders require a stove as part of the sale. Check out Sears Outlets for appliances at discount prices. Look for appliances with scratches and dents on the side which will be concealed by a wall or cabinetry.

The stove is the kitchen's focal point.
Accentuate the stove with tile surrounds or paint embellishments on the walls to make this area prominently shine.

If your doghouse has a repulsive looking refrigerator either throw it away or dress up the front. The inside must be cleanable before wasting time on the front. Buyers don't expect a refrigerator in many locales, but they do in Florida. If it is not customary to include a refrigerator in your area, taking it out increases the visual space in your kitchen.

Brian took a $50.00 ugly refrigerator, applied wood strips with a brad nail gun, and built a wall next to it. This built-in refrigerator at Sugar Plum Cabin is now an excellent feature. We borrowed space from the dining room next to the kitchen and built a pantry opposite the refrigerator. This enlarged the tiny kitchen. Brian extended the kitchen linoleum into the dining room to line up with the refrigerator and the pantry. (See photo on page 139.)

Idyllic Bedrooms

Sugar Plum Main Bedroom, painted warm red for romance and drama

The main bedroom, decisive from a buyer's point of view, requires privacy, visual appeal, and impressive extras. Capitalize on exciting and luxurious amenities. You want the main bedroom to feel relaxing, inviting, and restful. Highlight open space or create visual space with mirrors, landscape paintings, and decorative paint finishes. If you hang a painting or mirror in an unfurnished room and it looks out of place, try setting a potted plant, simple shelf, or chair under the wall hanging.

Keep secondary bedrooms simple and allow the buyers imaginations to fill the space with their needs. Paint the walls in a light color that blends with the main living space for a whole-house harmonious feeling. Add a large painting or mirror to increase small spaces visually, with a small chair to the side under the prop. A large up-lighted plant brings fascinating shadows into play.

Mask unsightly views with light-filtering window coverings. Think privacy and restful serenity. Window coverings also add softness to unfurnished bedrooms with all hard surfaces. Window hardware supplements architectural details and brings interest to plain rooms.

Bedrooms require few props; don't overfill with personal accessories. Buyers visualize their own furnishings according to their needs. Your goal is to supplement the bedroom with just enough design detail to bring about desired emotional response and to create visual stimulation in an otherwise humdrum room.

If plan to sell in spring or summer and your air conditioning needs a little help, install ceiling fans in the bedrooms. Make sure the ceiling can hold the weight first. Appreciated by buyers, ceiling fans additionally supplement the emotional ambiance with gentle breezes that convey the desired feeling of rest and relaxation.

Bathrooms that Sell

Cleanliness is crucial in bathrooms. Take down dingy shower curtains and window coverings. We use Restore4 to clean up unsightly bathtubs, sinks, and toilets. The pool chemical muriatic acid also cleans up hideous toilet rings. Replace cracked toilets and sinks, unsightly medicine cabinets, and leaky or ugly faucets. Kill mold and mildew with bleach or TSP. Use caution and provide plenty of ventilation with caustic cleaners. Refinish discolored bathtubs if Restore4 leaves blemishes. Cheaper than replacement, this expense is well worth the investment.

For bathrooms with little wood molding, light or cream colored walls look clean and bright. If nice wood molding and cabinetry exists, paint the wood gloss white, and then paint the walls a soft, bright color. This makes the woodwork stand out and the bathroom appears more out of the ordinary than bathrooms painted all white.

Other accessories and props multiply your sale proceeds. Use bright lighting along with large mirrors. You don't need to replace the shower curtain, but window coverings add privacy and design details. Also, curtains mask unattractive views of neighboring side walls.

Get imaginative with towel bars—we painted PVC plumbing pipe silver and hung it with small brass chains at Sugar Plum Cabin. Brian fashioned towel bars and toilet paper holders out of tree branches at Bell Pond. Fluffy towels insert a soft texture to the hard surface space, plus they supplement color, and you get to take them with you.

A simple accessory such as this towel rack adds visual interest for little expense.

Hot Water and Cool Air

The water heater and heating and air conditioning systems need to function properly. Get help from an expert at a large discount plumbing supply for contractors. We believed that the furnace at Bell Pond didn't work. Evan surprised us by fixing it with a small part recommended by the counter person at the contractor's supply who explained the repair.

If your dollhouse needs a new system, offer this as part of your sale and get it done in escrow to delay expense. Many contractors will do the work and send the bill to your escrow company for payment. Contractors know that if the sale falls through, they can put a lien on the property and get paid at a later sale or refinance.

Rejoice!

You've finished your hard work and the transformation is complete! Take "after" photographs and document your improvements.

Throw a party before advertising or listing your investment property. Invite your dollhouse neighbors and their friends and family as well as your contacts. You might sell your dollhouse during this party without any further advertising.

Invitation

> **Your presence is requested at Jeanette & Brian's Dollhouse Party.**
> Come view our latest project and celebrate with us!
> Please bring any friends looking for a new home.
> Sunday afternoon, noon to four.

Keep Your Dollhouse Sparkling Clean

To keep your floors in excellent condition, request a "no shoes" policy. We provide hospital booties to slip on over shoes for those who prefer not to go barefoot. Pick up a box of these at your local medical supply store.

Now that you have finished your transformation, get ready for the fun of staging your dollhouse to sell for maximum profits.

Chapter Seven

Selling for Maximum Profit

Buy your next doghouse now. Since it takes time and effort to find your next doghouse, start looking as soon as you finish your dollhouse. If you find a bargain house to purchase through a go-getter real estate agent, list your dollhouse with this agent. Your listing and purchase give double motivation to your agent to sell your dollhouse quickly. Try to do concurrent escrows with the same escrow company, negotiate a savings in escrow fees, and transfer profits from one property directly into the new property. This final step offers tax advantages—ask your accountant about a tax-free exchange.

Advantages of a Selling Agent

Even if you screen your buyers before showing your dollhouse, you never truly know what kind of person you invite into your home. If strangers scare you or intimidate you, listing your dollhouse solves this problem. Take into account the value of your time: instead of devoting energy on selling your dollhouse, you could be looking for your next unburied treasure—a doghouse waiting for transformation.

The main reason to list your dollhouse with an agent is protection. Many real estate agents even list their own homes with another agent just for shelter against future lawsuits. For those not savvy about local real estate customs and contract laws, listing with a knowledgeable agent is invaluable.

Smart agents know experts who charge less and save you money. These contacts are priceless. For instance, agents know appraisers who give the appraisal you deserve for your hard work, honest termite inspectors, lenders who act quickly, and escrow companies with great officers. Build a file of contacts to use when you branch out and go for sale by owner. When you feel comfortable with the sales process, you can make the sales commission yourself.

You still have work to do even if you list your dollhouse with an agent. Make a list of all your property's features and amenities, then research market sales prices. Busy agents won't spend the time detailing your flyer and they are not as familiar with the property. One of my listing agents forgot to mention our property was lakefront! Also, double-check your agent's proposed sales price with similar homes currently on the market.

Find a listing agent who promises to accompany selling agents to show your property. Teach your agent how you want the property shown. This is more important if there is a problem with the floor plan. If your dollhouse shows well on its own, let buyers ramble around on their own. Too many bodies make small houses even more crowded and buyers feel more comfortable viewing the property without the owner present.

Also, find an agent willing to set the stage for showing. Make a diagram of lights you want turned on and specify the temperature for the thermostat. Many listing agents just rely on the multiple listing service and other agents to sell and don't bother to take the time to open your house for showing.

Sometimes it's better if you show the house yourself. This way, you assure that the house is prepared for showing the way you want it and you know how to direct the prospective buyers through for best viewing.

One problem with listing your house is you get lax about the showing of your dollhouse. Ask the selling agent to make an appointment with you so you can set the house up the way it looks best. If you perform all this work, ask the listing agent for a commission discount.

Bear in mind, if the listing agent doesn't do much work and falls back on promises to you, you can renegotiate the commission when you are presented with an offer lower than your listing price. Point out that the agent paid less for advertising, you prepared the property for showing, and you think it's unfair for them to collect three percent of the selling price, which is much higher than your equity portion. Offer three percent of your profit instead or a one percent commission on the sales price. After all, the buyer's agent brought the competent buyer.

Advantages of Selling by Owner

Can you really save money selling by owner? Yes you can, if you are tough and the real estate market moves quickly. Keep in mind; you give up your free time and must be available at the drop of a hat to show your property. Think of the process as making money instead of saving money. You complete all the work the real estate agents normally perform for the commission.

Important Warning!
Pick out a prospective lender. The seller has the right in California and in other states to approve the lender and the escrow company. Interview lenders until you find one who acts reasonably, quickly, and offers easy qualifications. Primarily important to your sale is the lender's appraiser. Avoid banks that have a tendency to use appraisers who undercut the value. Once we let buyers use Bank of America because the buyers were pre-qualified with their bank, but we lost $13,000 in this sale because of an under-value appraisal.

Also, find a nearby escrow office and interview an officer. Avoid driving a long distance to sign papers or to pick up your check. Ask about the escrow office policy regarding when you get your funds. Many Realtors with in-house escrow companies like to hold up final disbursement for a couple of days; whereas smaller companies usually release funds promptly after close of escrow. If you want your proceeds immediately, give escrow wiring instructions to your bank a few days before close of escrow. Banks provide forms with wiring instructions or give the long list of numbers over the telephone. Some banks refuse to release funds from a wire transfer the same day, but most wait only four hours. Our bank holds certified funds over $5,000 for a few days, even an escrow check drawn from their bank!

Sales Price

Go online and look at properties listed on Realtor.com or MLS using the zip code. Enter the number of bedrooms, bathrooms, and pertinent information. Make a list of properties similar to yours and drive by these houses. Compare the square footage and curb appeal. Imagine you are a buyer in this market. Which property would you choose? Hopefully yours! If you find many of these listings already sold, this indicates a hot market for selling.

Call your title insurance company and request a property profile with comps (comparable sales) on your dollhouse. Note the most recent sale prices and checkout these properties. Drive around the neighborhood and pick up flyers for other homes for sale.

Price your property according to the competition, not out-of-date sales. The real estate market in California moves so fast, many Realtors will give you comparable sales that are *old news*. Appraisers use recent sales and market prices to value your property. Find the statistics on most recent sales and comparable listings. Give these comps to your appraiser, real estate agents, and potential buyers.

Don't overprice your dollhouse. Be realistic and take into account that buyers know what else is out there. Overpricing costs you money in many ways. You slow down the sale and you incur additional costs. You delay purchasing your next investment property and miss out on promising profits.

Build in Buyer's Costs

Ask your lender and escrow officer for a list of expected costs to close escrow. If you list your home, your Realtor is supposed to give you an estimated closing statement listing your costs and estimated cash out. It is common in California for an offer to exceed the listed price to include the buyer's costs when the buyer possesses insufficient funds to close without the seller's help. When you know the buyer's estimated costs, you can add these to your sales price if you sell by owner. Depending on the buyer's costs, offer your property in a price range instead of just one price. For instance, "dollhouse offered from $199,900 to $209,900—possible zero down OAC" (On Approved Credit). The lower price indicates a sale where the buyers pay their own costs and the higher price indicates a sale with the seller paying the buyer's costs.

Sales Contracts

Pick up a few standard sales contracts from your local Board of Realtors to make available when showing the property. Also get a full disclosure statement to give the buyer. Study these forms so that you learn how to fill them out quickly. Complete the form in advance with property address, legal description, your name, and any areas you prefer not to budge on.

Talk to Your Lenders and inform them about your property, which you want to sell right away. Ask for advice on current available loans for first-time home buyers. Find out if they offer a zero down program or the minimum down payment requirement. Get specific details on the estimated closing costs and monthly payment expense. Estimate the buyer's new property tax and home owner's insurance cost. Look for a lender who allows you to offer your dollhouse with zero down and seller paying buyer's closing costs. Find the most flexible lender for "B & C" (lower credit scores) buyers to enlarge your potential market.

Be sure to talk to your lenders about their appraisers. You need an appraisal crediting you with all your hard work. Some appraisers decline crediting your improvements and use *your purchase price* as the basis for a new appraisal. You definitely don't want an appraisal coming in lower than your selling price! Buyers usually balk at paying more than the appraised amount.

Orange Tree Cottage needed two appraisals before we got a high enough appraisal. Thank goodness

the buyers didn't change their minds and cancel
the sale after the first lower appraisal. The first
appraiser sent an assistant out to measure and
photograph the property. Then the appraiser just
used our purchase price as his basis since it was
so recent. This is why you must use a lender with
flexible appraisers.

Effective Advertising

Flyers

Make your sale flyer first. This will help you be
concise in your newspaper ads. List all the
amenities, features, and create an appealing
headline. Use the best photo of just your house,
cutting off neighboring houses. List your price
range and offer to help buyers with costs. Or, put
in the minimum down and the monthly
payments, such as Zero Down, $1,500 per month.

To make your flyer set your computer margins,
including top and bottom, as wide as possible.
Make your heading bold, beautiful, and
emphasize the best feature of your location or
property. Use your nickname for your dollhouse
next in smaller print followed by a good, clear,
color photograph. Under the photograph make
two columns listing all the benefits to your buyer,
property features and upgrades. Finally, list your
price and best terms in bold and big print to
balance the top of the flyer. Include "Easy
Qualifying" and "OAC" (On Approved Credit) to
protect yourself from those who will try to get you
to finance, claiming your flyer said they could

have the home for no money down, or whatever terms offered, with you acting as the bank.

Distribute flyers around the neighborhood and invite neighbors to a showing. Neighbors frequently know someone looking for a home. My Realtor friend Ruth always got her leads by working the neighborhood and distributing business cards with the address, bedroom count, down payment, and monthly payment.

Newspapers

Local newspapers cost less for advertising than big-market newspapers. Think about how you would find a house for sale in your target market area. Would you pick up all newspapers or just one? If someone desperately needs a home, they get all the newspapers, free bulletins, Penny Savers, and real estate brochures available. Pick up these ads and look through them. What attracts your eye? Whatever appeals to you should also catch the attention of your potential buyers.

Signs

Along with flyers, prominent signs in the front yard sell most homes. Hire a sign painter to make a sign, which says "3 Bedroom Home." Avoid the word "house." List any remarkable features like pool or view. The phrase "for sale by owner" is a powerful selling feature to some potential buyers who think they will secure a better deal without an agent. Creating a generic sign with your phone number allows you to reuse the sign on your next venture.

Attach a box next to your sign for your flyers.
Keep this box well-stocked but don't put too many
flyers in at a time. Some looky-lou's take the
entire stack and you quickly run out of flyers.
One frantic unqualified buyer tried to keep us
from selling to someone else and we caught him
taking all the flyers. Our posters around town
constantly disappeared as well.

Directional signs

Home improvement centers carry plastic signs
with little metal stands. These work better than
using telephone poles, as the city or county
removes illegally posted signs. Look for signs with
a directional arrow and space for personalization,
like phone number and address. Serious
homebuyers look at properties with an agent and
then drive around areas of interest to them. This
is why direction signs and flyers at the property
help sell most houses.

Internet Ads

I follow Internet ads looking for bargain houses.
Some real estate Internet sites provide free
advertising to owner-sellers. I used one of these
sites to list a dollhouse and I still get investor
emails and calls a year later. However, with the
rising market, this free ad doesn't help because
the price of houses increased drastically. That
$159,000 property now comps out at $239,000.

Open Houses

Real estate agents use open houses to meet
prospective buyers and rarely sell the open house.
If you decide to try an open house remember that

your time equals money, so go to the expense of advertising and stay available for telephone calls and showings.

The exception to this "Open House" guideline is your party at the completion of your work. Invite your friends, family, and especially the dollhouse neighbors. Word of mouth, always a terrific selling tool, helps you beyond this particular sale. When people know what you do for extra income, they contact you for a home, or with a property for sale.

Receiving Telephone Calls
Prepare yourself for many Realtor calls trying to get the listing. Tell them you already promised the listing and they will stop bugging you. Or tell them to go ahead and bring a buyer, you'll consider all offers, and you pay the selling commission of three percent. This statement weeds out misrepresenting agents without "hot" buyers.

Try to screen out investors who call on all for-sale-by owners. They attempt to get you to carry back paper—be the bank—and refuse to pay what you deserve. Showing your property to investors wastes your valuable time. Ask the caller where they live now and when they expect to move. Any hesitancy will most likely mean you are talking to an investor. Also, investors try to monopolize the call by asking you questions and give you little information about their situation. When investors call, tell them you are an investor too and you expect a good return for your money and hard work.

Seek out a buyer looking for a personal home. These motivated buyers pay you the most money. After you establish the caller's intentions, find out more information about them and take notes. Friendly conversation and your excitement about your dollhouse lead to potential buyers viewing your property. Take note of their name and phone number. Tell them you need the phone number in case something comes up and you need to reschedule your appointment. People like hearing their name in conversation, so remember to use it often.

Most buyers today use a Realtor and many calls you receive will be from unqualified buyers. This is why you need a "B & C" lender friend. Undemanding lenders may help you sell your dollhouse to buyers dropped by real estate agents who are so busy they only work with "A" buyers.

Now that you understand credit issues, offer to help desperate buyers with their credit problems and they might buy your next property. Build a list of potential buyers and good tenants.

Remember, you deserve a good profit for all your hard work. Learn this saying by heart: *it only takes **one** buyer to sell your home.*

Staging Your Creation

"Set the stage" by emphasizing your property's desirable features and using psychology to increase your real estate profits. This vital phase of selling your investment property is what makes all the difference in getting paid the most for your real estate business.

Dress the Part
First of all, buyers may not buy your dollhouse if they don't like you. Change your grubby work clothes or "dress for success suit." Avoid looking messy or intimidating. Keep in mind the colors surrounding you in your dollhouse and don't wear clashing colors. You want the buyers to look at your creation, not at you.

Arrive at your dollhouse a few minutes earlier than your prospective buyers. Park your vehicle away from the front of the house. Calm any barking dogs. Tell neighbors you wish to get them the best new neighbors and ask them to please help by keeping their dogs quiet. Walk around outside and pick up any trash that may have appeared on or near your property.

Stage the Setting
If it is cold outside, turn on all the lights and start a fire in the fireplace. During hot weather, turn on the air conditioner and cool lights—a shady shelter feels refreshing. Turn on light fixtures you want to emphasize that stay with the property and any extra lighting that enhances the viewing.

Air the house out. You may need to crank the air conditioner or heater for a few minutes. The inside temperature should be around 68 degrees in the summer and 70 degrees in the winter.

Listen to the neighborhood noises. Mask any unpleasant sounds with music. If the neighborhood is quiet, you want to point this out by leaving the music off.

Run water in the sinks to clear pipes and traps of unpleasant odors. Flush toilets. Every inch needs to be immaculate and neat. Check paintings and mirrors to make sure they hang in a straight line. Dust off window sills, mantles, shelves, and any furnishings. Throw-away gloves for this purpose make this job quick and easy.

Take cuttings from your garden. Use available flowers or cut stems from bushes or trees. Make sure to cut plants with pleasant scents and steer clear of unpleasant odors. Stay away from oleander or other plants which affect many people's allergies. Buyers won't buy a house they're allergic to!

Review your checklist for showing (see appendix D) and don't forget something in your haste and excitement. Watch for prospective buyers to arrive and direct them to park in a place that doesn't detract from viewing the property. Encourage the buyers to park in the best space for the maximum benefit. Don't let the buyers drive right up to the front door—it isn't pleasant to look out from the living room and see cars.

Evan and Natalie's Remodeled Bathroom with dramatic foliage for staging. (Notice the way Evan hid the plumbing behind a new wall and created a shelf.)

Showing to Sell

Show your dollhouse during the best part of the day. Take advantage of the sunlight or sunset. Our Valley View Ranch displayed a spectacular sunset view and also twilight obscured the neighbor's messy yard.

We leave a basket of surgical booties at the front door of our dollhouses for buyers coming to look. The extra care pleases buyers and the booties keep the floors spotless.

Plan your traffic pattern—the best way to show off your property. Practice showing the property to a friend. Learn to let the other person go first so you don't block the line of vision. This also makes the space appear larger. Walk behind the buyers and direct the flow by telling them which way to go. Figure out the best way to proceed through the home. Try to show the "public rooms" first and the bedrooms last. The direction should make the most of the floor plan. Remember the example of Valley View Ranch with the strange layout? We showed the home by walking outside from the laundry room, around the back yard, and then back into the bedroom from the backyard.

Emphasize the highlights and minimize time spent in less desirable areas. Steer clear of bragging about all the hard work you completed. Be proud of your work and creation, but emphasize the outcome, not the work details. Point out new features and tell the buyers you offer flexible terms. Telling them this fundamental finance feature upfront gets their minds working towards a purchase.

After the initial walk-through, let the buyers investigate by themselves and give them a chance to talk in private. Leave them in a pleasing room for a few minutes. Interested buyers look around more and then they come to you. If you hear them talking about where their furniture goes, you have most likely made a sale.

Invite the buyers to join you at the table for coffee, tea, or water. Ask them what they think about the home. Pull out a notebook and take notes. Be a little assertive—after all you created a wonderful setting and they need a home. Otherwise, you get nowhere by talking forever. Ask how much they have saved for a down payment and offer your built-in buyer's costs at this time. Ask: "what if you could get into this home for only $2,000"? Always say "*home.*" Your arrangement with your lender aids you in understanding currently available financing. If your buyers have $5,000 handy, they will be thrilled to keep $3,000.

If the buyers don't make an offer, remember that most buyers need a few days to think about a major purchase. When buyers call back for another appointment—this is the time to press for commitment. If the buyer doesn't call you—call them and ask if they've found a home yet. Invite them to come back and take another look at your home.

Be prepared for looky-lou's who waste your time and for investors who insult you. Looky-lou's, curious people who like to see houses, are not serious buyers. Some unkind investors think they need to run down a property to get a better price. Let their negativity and ignorance go. Don't allow anyone to manipulate you or cause you to lose faith in your creation.

Most buyers want you to discount the sale price by the real estate broker fee. Explain that you are an investor, you act as your own agent, and expect the same compensation; otherwise, you would list the property and let real estate agents do all the complicated work.

You must have a contract with a deposit check to hold your dollhouse. Ask for at least one percent deposit. Open escrow with a minimum amount, but fill in the space on the contract where the deposit increases after the home inspection. Let the buyers pay for a home inspection if they ask for one, but sell the house "as is" and limit your repair costs in the termite report section. Tell them about home warranties which cover unexpected repairs. Only pay for this expense if they insist.

In some states, you must also give the buyers a full disclosure. No need to scare them off with this during the sales contract signing phase; execute this document in escrow.

Important! Check out your buyer's proposed lender and escrow company before agreeing to any offer. Avoid unknown lenders whenever possible. You need a full value appraisal and a firm loan commitment, not just a pre-qualifying statement. Most escrow companies or closing services perform well, but you need one close to home. You want a quick escrow or you will lose money paying more mortgage payments. Offer an incentive to the buyer to close within 30 days. Tell the buyers you will leave the "prop" they love if they close on time. Buyer's concessions, motivated by some little enticement, cost you less than a long escrow.

Offers to Refuse

Investors come up with all kind of schemes to buy your dollhouse. Do not let them talk you into assuming your loan. Imagine what if's...What if the investor rents the house to horrible tenants who destroy your hard work? What if the investor collects the rent and defaults on the loan? Investors with little outlay position themselves with little to lose—but you stand to lose your nest egg.

> ## Be patient for the right buyer.

Selling Escrow

Keep showing the house during the first week of escrow. Many unexpected things happen to make sales fall apart. One of our qualified buyers who passed my lender's pre-qualification owed thousands of dollars for child support and the sale fell through. Buyers change their minds, say they lost their job, or buy a new car... Realtors term this phase "buyer's remorse." Any disqualification in obtaining their loan means the buyers get their deposit back. Continue to show the property, keep new prospect's phone numbers, and take back-up offers.

Follow your selling escrow checklist (see appendix B). Talk to the real estate agents or buyers, lender, and escrow officer often to avert potential problems. Reassure the buyers that they made a good choice. Stay on top of the details to ensure a timely closing. Call at least once a week and more often if a problem arises. Follow your selling escrow checklist and monitor the steps. Help arrange termite inspections, home inspections, and appraisals without delay to ensure a timely closing.

Selling Appraisal

You absolutely must meet the buyer's appraiser at the property. Depending on someone else to stage the setting on this most important date can make you lose lots of money. Your dollhouse must flaunt its glorious metamorphosis with your help.

Prominently display your transformation photo album and show the appraiser the work involved and expenses incurred. Detailed "before" photographs substantiate the property's previous conditions as compared to the final result. Keep your receipts of materials used in your workbook handy to show the appraiser. Avoid possible complications with your sale by showing the appraiser all the improvements made to the property to get your deserved upgraded appraisal. This is crucial—the appraiser must give you credit for your work and expenses and not use your recent purchase price as market value. This is the time to brag about all your hard work.

Closing Escrow

Follow the details of your selling escrow and make certain all the service providers, such as lenders, escrow officers, and real estate agents do their jobs in order. Congratulate yourself on close of escrow! Celebrate that your dollhouse will give joy to its new owners, and a well-deserved paycheck to you.

Chapter Eight

Holding for Your Future Income

Rather than flipping every property, you may want to keep your dollhouse as a rental to secure future income and profit. My daughter says this is a brilliant way to take out a loan and have someone else pay it off!

It is best to determine before your transformation if you intend to keep your dollhouse. Since single family home rentals are so challenging to find in many Southern California cities, renters pay high prices for houses that even need work. The transformation plan for a "keeper" differs from that of a dollhouse for dollars.

The real estate business offers many choices and opportunities. Instead of selling your improved property, most likely the property now qualifies for a refinance of the mortgage or a second loan to get out most of your equity. Keep in mind you need adequate cash to buy your next real estate project.

Think of it this way. You sell a dollhouse for $200,000 and receive $40,000. You then buy a doghouse for $200,000, put $20,000 down, have the sellers pay your closing costs, and pocket $20,000. Or you refinance your dollhouse, receive a check for $30,000, put $20,000 into your next project, and pocket $10,000. You now have two investment properties. Or, consider selling your first dollhouse and use most of your money for two down payments on two investment properties.

Cash Flow

Before you decide to keep your investment property, consider your cash flow. Calculate expenses such as your mortgage and interest payments, insurance, taxes, and maintenance expenses. Compare to projected rental income and decide if you can afford any difference.

Refinance to get your investment money back and open a bank account specifically for this property. Pay any negative out of this fund. We got an easy "Home Equity Line of Credit" from our bank on Sugar Plum Cabin with no fees and no appraisal. I filled out the application online, the bank looked at the property profile which looked at the previous sale (the one prior to our purchase) and allotted this price as the basis. This property was a HUD—we purchased it for $110,000 yet the previous sale price was $179,000. We got more money from the loan proceeds than our down payment, closing costs, and transformation costs. In my mind, because it pays for itself, we own a free mountain cabin!

Properties to Keep or Sell
Keep houses that won't cause problems for you and sell houses with features easily ruined by tenants. Light colored carpeting gets stained and most likely destroyed. Properties with delicate features, like those with doors featuring stained

glass windows, expensive wallcoverings, spas, and/or fragile landscaping make poor rental candidates. In contrast, houses with resilient features like block-wall construction, sturdy windows, hardy landscaping, and no swimming pools make better rental properties.

Becoming a landlord can be either a blessing or a nightmare. For easier dealings with tenants, act as the representative of your real estate investment company instead of the owner. When you first meet the prospective tenant, tell them you represent XYZ investments and you follow their guidelines. This way, you avoid feeling obligated to listen hardship sob stories, becoming involved with your tenants' personal life, and thereby relaxing your rental requirements. (You will need a business checking account to have the tenants make their check out to.)

Tenants

Finding good tenants is tricky. Avoid personal contact by hiring a leasing agency to handle your property, or make the extra money by using their techniques. Get applications from an office supply store. Require prospective tenants to fill out the last *two* landlords. The current landlord may want to get rid of the tenants and not share the complaint list with you. The more cooperative prior landlords share complete complaint details. When you call previous landlords, use the phrase "complaint lists." Use caution: savvy renters list relatives as previous landlords to get a good recommendation. Make sure your lease or rental agreement contains a permissive clause to run credit and run prospective tenant's credit history. Ask your lender for help with this.

Give a few dollars off the rent for prompt payment and add a penalty charge to late payments. For instance, rent is $1,500 per month due on the first, discounted to $1,475 if paid before the 1st, and $1,650 if paid after the 3rd. This incentive ensures prompt payment to you and discourages late payments with a large fine. Check your local landlord laws before adding this clause as some areas regulate landlords heavily.

Write into the rental agreement what pets, if any, you permit. List all tenants and exclude any additional people moving in. Avoid other family members moving in, like a situation we encountered: a grown daughter returned home with a new boyfriend and two children to join our tenants, already a family of five.

Evan's Theory on Value

Renters buy your property for you. Market fluctuations make little difference—the property ultimately increases tremendously in value. Even if property values temporarily decline, don't worry as the prices will eventually go up again.

Living in Your Investment Property

It is a shame that you can avoid taxes by selling your own home and reinvesting the profit in your next home. Many investors buy homes and trade up every two years just to circumvent high taxation. (Because of property taxes, in reality, you never truly own any property; you just rent it from the government.)

Buy Two Properties

Split your profit and buy two houses. Try to get a longer escrow on one. The property value should increase while you are not even paying for it. This is what we did after selling Orange Tree Cottage— we bought Sugar Plum Cabin and Valley View Ranch at the same time with a longer escrow on the one purchased from the owner.

We used the same mortgage broker to do this. He placed the loans with different banks at the same time. This way, we only had to qualify once for two purchases and only had our credit run one time.

If you sell one dollhouse and keep one, buy two more, sell one and keep one, and buy two more... you'll be on your way to securing a great nest egg that no other investment strategy can promise.

Retire with Passive Income

Make a long-term plan according to your current age and desired retirement age. Determine how many rentals you need to receive your desired income. If you dream of retiring now with $10,000 per month, how many rentals would you need paid down or off? Let's assume ten. The actual income should inflate in line with inflation. So in twenty years the income should have the same purchasing power as it does today.

How do you get ten rentals paid off in 20 years? Finance your rentals for twenty years, decreasing the financing time for each subsequent property, or buy three doghouses, sell two and pay down the retained rental. Keep doing this until you pay off your rentals.

Another income and early retirement option is to buy two doghouses at a time; sell one for profit and added income for that year and buy two more.

Five-Year Retirement Plan

Year 1	Buy first doghouse, transform and sell. Buy second doghouse; sell and buy two, sell one and keep one	Total Rentals
		1
Year 2	Buy two doghouses, and sell one	2
	Buy two doghouses, and sell one	3
Year 3	Buy two doghouses, and sell one	4
	Buy two doghouses, and sell one	5
Year 4	Buy two doghouses, and sell one	6
	Buy two doghouses, and sell one	7
Year 5	Buy two doghouses, and sell one	8
	Buy two doghouses, and sell one	9

This plan gives you three dollhouses to sell during the first year to give you a financial boost and two properties during each succeeding year for sales profits. After *five* years you will have nine rentals! Once you develop your own successful investment strategy, you should pick up another rental on your way to financial freedom, giving you ten rentals. If you choose not to work so hard, spread the plan out over ten years.

At this point, you have many options:

- Enjoy the rental cash flow
- Sell your problem properties for cash
- Keep buying and selling
- Exchange your rental houses for apartments
- Sell a few rentals and pay the rest off
- Refinance

Refinancing for Cash Flow

In five years, refinance the first income property. This borrowed money isn't considered income by the IRS and is not taxed until you sell. Every six months after, refinance the next property for cash flow. The first property purchased should have appreciated enough to refinance, still pay for itself, and get your equity out TAX FREE! You possibly could refinance each property in line of purchase every six months for the rest of your life. Hopefully, the rental income will increase sufficiently to cover the higher payments of the refinancing. This refinancing plan certainly works best if you purchase each property below market value and increase its sales price or rental income by fixing it up.

Investor's Tips

The physician can bury his mistakes, but the architect can only advise his client to plant vines. – Frank Lloyd Wright

I've gathered the following tips from my family and some of my most successful investor contacts. These include other examples and strategies that may interest you in addition to transforming a doghouse into dollars.

Brian's Tips
Land is a rich person's investment with no income and no tax shelter. Eighty percent of Americans desire their own single-family detached home and only fifty percent do. Single family, detached homes are easy to find, easy to finance, and easy to sell. Find the dirtiest dog in the best neighborhood and turn it into the champion.

Bob's Tips
Turn $10,000 into a million dollars in five years. Buy the vacant land on a main road next to a vacant large corner parcel near an expanding area. When a major business develops the corner, your little piece next door increases in value— some times more than ten times the purchase price. Try to get owner financing with low payments, at least for the first couple of years.

Karen's Tips
Buy fourplexes and use property managers. Upgrade units and increase rental rates. Trade up to apartment complexes and seek owner financing, which is often available with these purchases as the wealthy investor-sellers need less cash.

John's Tips
Buy a two bedroom, one bathroom house in a good neighborhood with larger and more expensive houses. Add on a Master Bedroom with

a great bathroom. You should be able to sell the property for the higher price of the larger and more expensive neighboring homes.

Buy one bedroom apartments in Section 8 housing. Your rent is guaranteed by the government for a steady stream of income. No need to worry about partying tenants and destructive children—one bedroom is so small the tenants are usually the elderly.

Rob's Tips
For married couples applying separately for property financing: set up individual credit and checking accounts. Use the appropriate checking account for your deposit check as the lender may ask escrow for a copy of this check and you want to avoid potential problems.

Fran's Tips
Location—Buy the best location possible. Acceleration Clause: Be sure to include an acceleration clause in any financing you provide. Fran has seen many investor-friends lose "their little shirts" because they forgot this essential clause which makes the loan payable when the property is resold.

Joanie's Tips
Buy many VA repos in outlying areas. Use vendee financing—the financing provided from the VA (you don't need to be a vet for this, but this is not always available). The VA usually fixes their homes just enough so it is easy to get financing. These homes are very low down with little escrow

costs. There isn't as much bidding competition to get houses in outlying areas. Lease out the property and hold for long term. Eventually, you will receive a lot of cash flow for retirement.

When you refinance for cash, get your own appraisal using someone you know first. Then ask the bank to do an appraisal review. Even though this costs a little more, you usually get a higher appraisal.

Evan's Tips

Buy new homes in a large development as soon as they are offered for sale but before they are built. By the time the project is finished and as each phase increases in price, you have earned increased value without any work. Plus, you don't have to close escrow right away, and therefore you have only used your cash for the deposit until you actually close, by which time you have earned all the increases.

Mark's Tips

Jump into the stream. Without a property, you're not even in the river. Buy a home and live in it for two years and then refinance it, use the cash to buy another house for yourself with similar payments. This way, you have a rental and a better home for yourself with no increased monthly payments if the rent covers the rental.

If you sell your personal home every few years and put the entire equity into the next home or increase your payments a little, you keep moving up into nicer houses.

(This advice is contrary to many wealthy investors who advocate spending less money for housing needs. Larger, costlier residences increase housing expenses, and change lifestyles, thereby swelling everyday expenditures needlessly. Luxury homes demand luxury automobiles, lavish clothing, and extravagant trappings, which don't always bring happiness.)

Starting Capital

Find a really trashed house and ask the seller for short term or temporary financing. Point out that the expenses and labor to bring the house up to sale condition count as your down payment. Or, ask the seller to equity share with you. You do the work and the seller pays for materials. Get a deed for half ownership in exchange for your labor. Split the profits after the sale.

Another way to get investment capital is to ask an owner of distressed property for a mortgage note payable to you in increased increments as your work on the house progresses. Make the notes payable on sale and you get paid when the fixed-up house sells.

Free Housing for College Students

Many business majors in college now invest in property to apply what they learn to a real-life situation. This can be both an educational and profitable undertaking for your college student.

Find a doghouse near campus and purchase as owner occupant with no money down and seller paying closing costs. You may need to put your student on title for lender occupancy requirements. Prior planning for your student's good credit standing helps with financing, but it is not necessary for taking title. Fix up the property, refinance with a Home Equity Line of Credit, and open a bank account to pay expenses. Rent out extra bedrooms to students with parents who guarantee rent (and perhaps your own college student will live rent-free!). When the student graduates, sell the property and receive a paycheck, or keep as a rental for continued income.

Choose Your Individual Investment Strategy

You find more happiness doing what you love and you make more money if you enjoy what you're doing. Choose ideas from successful investors to adopt and reinvent them for your specific desires. Develop your own investing strategy by repeating your achievements and become more successful following your own real estate investment model. Once you find a system which works for you—do it over and over again.

I hope you feel motivated, and sufficiently armed with knowledge and strategies, to begin your successful venture into the world of real estate investment. I hope you love the work as much as we do. I'm certain you'll enjoy the rewards of wealth and security. Go for it! Go buy a Doghouse! Turn your dream dollhouse into reality!

Appendix
Step-by-Step Checklist
1. Order copies of credit reports
2. Create Telephone Log
3. Create Mileage log
4. Learn local & second home real estate markets
5. Repair credit if needed as reports arrive
6. Interview Lenders
7. Interview Real Estate Agents
8. Shop around for property
9. Estimate transformation costs
10. Make lender decision
11. Make Offers
12. Open Escrow
13. Arrange fire insurance
14. Measure doghouse
15. Plan budget
16. Grow plants
17. Create Overall Design Plan
18. Create Landscape Plan
19. Design room by room work plan
20. Shop for materials
21. Arrange utilities
22. Close Escrow
23. Take "before" photographs
24. Check safety issues
25. Clean up
26. Celebrate with Open House
27. Gather supplies, tools, and building materials
28. Start work time log
29. Begin transformation
30. Landscaping
31. Exterior
32. Interior
33. Staging
34. Take "after" photographs
35. Celebration Party
36. Selling
37. Advertising
38. Showing checklist
39. Selling Escrow Checklist
40. Close Escrow & go to bank!

Escrow Checklist

Date escrow opened: Estimated closing date:

Deposit to be increased to: Date:

Escrow office:
Telephone Number:
Escrow officer:
Officer assistant:
Escrow number:
Seller:
Seller phone:
Listing agent: Phone:
Selling agent: Phone:
Title Company:
Fire Insurance provider:

Good-faith estimate from lender:
Preliminary title report received:
Appraisal ordered date:
Appraiser:
Appraiser phone:
Termite report:
Home inspection:
Commitment letter from lender:
Loan docs:
Funding:
Recording:
Dispersal:

Planning Budget

See Estimated costs of Materials page 82 and Workbook for complete worksheets

Paint:

Flooring
    Hard surfaces:
    Carpeting:

Kitchen
    Appliances:
    Countertops:
    Cabinets:
    Sink & faucet:

Landscaping:

Plumbing:

Electrical:

Problems needing addressing:

Estimated funds needed: $ _____

Funds available: $ _____
Credit available $ _____
    Company name:
    Company name:
    Company name:
Financing options
    Company name:
    Company name:

Checklist for Showing—Staging Your Dollhouse

Park in inconspicuous place
Quiet neighboring dogs
Turn on lights
Air house out
Spray air freshener if needed
Set thermostat to: ____
Listen for irritating noises; turn music on if needed
Replace drooping flowers or tree branches in vases
Walk around perimeter—pickup trash
Run water in faucets to clear waterline & traps
Flush toilets
Open windows & window coverings for natural light (unless masking unsightly view)
Sweep floors if needed
Vacuum if needed
Check window coverings to make sure they drape as desired
Check paintings and mirrors to make sure they're straight
Check all rooms and closets
Watch for prospective buyer to direct parking in the best location for viewing property and not blocking views from inside

Resources

ReStore
Habitat for Humanity
Partner Service Center
Habitat for Humanity International
121 Habitat St.
Americus, GA 31709-3498, USA
Telephone: (229) 924-6935, ext. 2551 or 2552
E-mail: publicinfo@hfhi.org

Home Depot
www.homedepot.com
(Check out their daily sale page)
1-800-553-3199

Lowe's
1-800-44LOWES (1-800-445-6937)

Jeanette Fisher's Newsletters
Credit Help! Tips newsletter comes your way each month
with tips from mortgage brokers, readers who share
successful strategies, and credit experts. The emphasis,
credit requirements for mortgage financing, helps you
finance real estate. However, if your goal is just improving
your credit score, *Credit Help Tips* will help you do that, too!
http://recredithelp.com/

Doghouse to Dollar$ Real Estate Tips
How to buy, fix, and sell houses for top dollar—fast!
Discover the difference Design Psychology makes in real
estate profits. Includes how to sell your home for top dollar
tips. http://doghousetodollhouse.com/

Joy to the Home Journal
Discover how Mother Nature guides your home decorating
to create an environment for your emotional needs. Explore
the innovative interior design ideas and find out why home
decorators can't wait for their next issue.
http:// joytothehome.com/

Glossary

Acceleration clause: A clause in a mortgage or deed which accelerates the loan making it all due and payable immediately, usually when the payments become past due to a certain time period or if the property is sold.

Adjustable rate mortgage (ARM): A mortgage with an interest rate that may fluctuate and change the payments, usually with a *ceiling, cap*, or top amount.

Amenity: A feature of the property that increases attractiveness or value to the buyer, which is not necessary to its use, such as a pond, garden, or view.

Amortization: Paying back the loan with interest over a set period of time.

Annual percentage rate (APR): The actual cost of a loan including interest, points, mortgage insurance, fees expressed in interest terms as a yearly rate.

Application: The formal document or form on which a loan request is made.

Application Fee: The fee that a mortgage lender charges to apply for a mortgage to cover processing costs.

Appraisal: A formal document prepared by a licensed appraiser stating the true market or replacement value of a property.

Appreciation: Market value increase due to changing market conditions and/or home improvements.

Appraiser: A person qualified by education, training, and experience to provide appraisals.

ARM: Adjustable Rate Mortgage: A mortgage with an interest rate that may fluctuate and change the payments, usually with a *ceiling, cap*, or top amount.

Assessor: A government official who determines property value for taxation.

Assumable mortgage: A mortgage loan that can be transferred to the new owner.

Balloon payment: A large payment payable prior to the mortgage being paid off due to an acceleration clause.

Board of Realtors: Association of real estate agents with standards for members which provides services to its affiliates.

Building codes: Regulations set by local, state and national guidelines for safety establishing minimum standards for building materials, design, and construction.

Capacity: The ability to make mortgage payments on time depending upon income and income stability, assets and reserves, and the amount of income each month that is available after housing costs, debts and other obligations.

Cash flow: The monthly profit spendable after paying total expenses.

Cash reserves: Lenders often require borrowers to have additional funds above the down payment and closing costs covering a set amount of monthly expenditures.

Certificate of title: Like a title insurance policy, guarantees a title to be free of liens and encumbrances and that the seller legally owns the property with rights to sell.

Closing (closing date): Formal sale of property and transfer of ownership. In some areas called settlement.

Closing Agent (escrow officer): A third party professional that coordinates closing-related activities, such as recording the closing documents and disbursing funds.

Closing costs: Paid at transfer of ownership, sometimes partially included in a purchase mortgage. Closing costs include all charges above the purchase price.

Collateral: Property which is pledged as security for a debt. In mortgages, the collateral is the land, the house, and improvements.

Concession: Item given or conceded in negotiating a transaction.

Conditions: Lender conditions come with the loan documents. If the borrower meets these *conditions*, the loan will fund. Buyer and seller *conditions* are the requirements or concessions listed in the sales agreement.

Conforming Loans: Loans that meet normal and customary conditions under a certain dollar amount.

Conventional lenders: Non-government lenders in private business.

Conventional loan: A loan not insured by the government.

Commitment Letter: A letter from your lender that states the amount of the mortgage, the number of years to repay the mortgage (the term), the interest rate, the loan origination fee, the annual percentage rate and the monthly charges.

Comps: Comparable sales prices in the target market area.

Corbels: A bracket of stone, wood, brick, or other building material, projecting from the face of a wall generally supporting a cornice, arch or hardware.

Creative financing: Non-conforming financing for either the borrower or the property. Many times the property is not up to the standards set by lending institutions. Some borrowers also need imaginative assistance to get financing.

Counter-offer: An offer made in return by the person who rejects the previous offer.

Debt-to-income ratio: Comparison of mortgage payment, including taxes, interest and insurance to total gross monthly income.

Deed: The formal document that transfers property title.

Deed-in-lieu: A deed given to the lender to avoid foreclosure.

Deed of Trust: A legal document in which the borrower conveys the title to a third party (trustee) to hold as security for the lender. After the loan is paid off, the trustee reconveys the deed to the borrower. If the borrower defaults on the loan, the trustee sells the property and pays the lender the mortgage debt.

Default: When a borrower can't pay the monthly payments, the loan is in "default."

Delinquency: Failure of a borrower to make payments on time.

Depreciation: A decline in the value of a house due to changing market conditions, decline of a neighborhood or lack of upkeep on a home.

Distressed Properties: Real estate that should have a bargain price because of lack of care, lack of money, divorce, job loss or transfer, death, or other hardship circumstances.

Earnest money deposit: Money given by buyer showing serious intent to purchase. It is returned if the offer is not accepted or the sale falls through according to purchase contact terms and forfeited if the buyer does not perform.

Equity: The value of ownership after all loans, costs and liens are paid. The amount left over credited to the seller or the market value less liabilities.

Escrow: In California and in many other states, real estate sales are handled by a third impartial party who collects all documents, contracts, and monies to close a sale. In some states, an attorney or a title company acts as closing agent.

Escrow Officers: The third party, trained agent who handles an escrow or closing.

Exclusive Listing: When a seller hires one real estate company to represent the seller. The real estate company may share the sale with other agents. If the owner sells the property himself, he still owes the real estate company a commission.

Fair market value: The price a willing, able buyer will pay a seller who is not under pressure to sell.

Fannie Mae: The Federal National Mortgage Association (FNMA) a federally regulated privately owned business who supplies lenders with funds for lending to borrowers.

Federal Housing Administration—FHA: Part of the Department of Housing and Urban Development.

First time homebuyer's option: Special financing for purchasing a first owner-occupant home.

Fixed-Rate Mortgage: A mortgage with an interest rate that does not change during the lifetime of the loan.

Flipping property: Buying property and reselling right away for profit.

Floor plan: A scale diagram of a room or building drawn as if seen from above, also the layout of a home.

Footprint: The surface space occupied by a structure or home.

Foreclosure: A legal proceeding by which a mortgage is foreclosed and the end result—a property labeled "foreclosure.

Freddie Mac: Authorized by U S Congress, the Federal Home Loan Mortgage Corporation, (FHLMC or Freddie Mac) provides a secondary market for residential mortgages. Investors buy a security issued by the Federal Home Loan Mortgage Corporation and secured by a pool of conventional home mortgages. Because the loans are government insured

Full documented loans: "Full doc" processing type of loans require proof of income, tax returns, bank statements and more from the borrower.

Funding time: The length of time needed by a lender to complete the loan.

Garbage fees: Costs added by a lending institution increasing loan costs to the borrower.

Gift Letter: A letter from a family member verifying that he/she gave you a certain amount of money as a gift and that you do not have to repay it.

Good-Faith Estimate: A written statement itemizing the approximate costs and fees for the mortgage.

Gross Monthly Income: The income you earn in a month before taxes and other deductions. Often includes rental income, self-employed income, alimony, child support, public assistance payments, and retirement benefits.

Health and safety codes: Governmental codes establishing minimum standards for occupancy usually followed by lender as mandatory for full financing.

Hidden costs: Additional costs added by lenders to increase the loan costs to the borrower.

Home Equity Line of Credit—HELOC: Pronounced "he lock." A second that has a line of credit with fluctuating balances and corresponding payments.

Home Inspection: A professional inspection of a home to review the condition of the property. Should include an assessment of the plumbing, heating and cooling systems, roof, electrical, foundation, and pest infestation.

Homeowner's policy (Homeowner's Insurance): A policy that protects homeowner and lender from fire or flood, which damages the structure of the house; or a liability, such as an injury to a visitor; or damage to personal property.

Housing Expense Ratio: The percentage of gross monthly income that pays for housing expenses.

HUD: The United States Department of Housing and Urban Development.

HUD-1 settlement statement: A final accounting of the costs of the mortgage transaction. It provides the sales price, and down payment, as well as the total settlement costs required from the buyer and seller.

Index: The published index of interest rates on a publicly traded debt security used to calculate the interest rate for an ARM. The index is usually an average of the interest rates on a particular type of security.

Inquiry: A request for a copy of your credit report. An inquiry occurs every time you fill out a credit application and/or request more credit. Too many inquiries on a credit report can lower your credit score.

Interest: The cost paid to borrow money. Interest is usually expressed as a percentage of the amount borrowed.

Joint compound: A substance similar to plaster used to cover seams or the heads of screws or nails in plasterboard.

Jumbo Loans: Higher balance loans, usually having higher interest.

Keogh Funds: A tax-deferred retirement-savings plan for small business owners or self-employed individuals who have earned income from their trade or business. Contributions to the Keogh plan are tax deductible.

Liabilities: Debts and other monetary obligations.

Lien: A claim or charge on property for payment of some debt. With respect to a mortgage, it is the right of the lender to take the title to your property if you do not make the payments due on the mortgage.

Loan Origination Fees: The fee paid to mortgage lenders for processing the mortgage application. This fee is usually in the form of points. One point equals 1% of the mortgage amount.

Loan to Value Ratio: Also **loan to cost ratio**

Lock-in rate: A written agreement guaranteeing a specific interest rate when a mortgage closes.

Margin: The amount (expressed as a percentage) added to the index for an ARM to establish the interest rate on each adjustment date.

Market Value: The current value based on what a willing purchaser would pay. The value determined by an appraisal is commonly used to determine market value.

Mortgage: The amount borrowed secured by a lien on property. In some states the term mortgage is also used to describe the document you sign to show that you have granted the lender a lien on your home; other states use a deed of trust document instead of a mortgage. It may also be used to indicate the amount of money borrowed, with interest

Mortgage Broker: An independent finance professional specializing in bringing together borrowers and lenders to make possible real estate mortgages.

Mortgage Insurance (MI or PMI): Insurance needed for mortgages with low down payments (usually less than 20% of the price of the home).

Mortgage Lender: The lender providing funds for a mortgage. Lenders also manage the credit and financial information review, the property and the loan application process through closing.

Mortgage Rate: The cost or the interest rate paid to borrow money to buy a house.

Multiple Listing Service—MLS: Listing service used by real estate agents to share their homes for sale.

Net Monthly Income: Your take-home pay after taxes. It is the amount of money that you actually receive in your paycheck.

Nonrecurring closing costs: Escrow fees and loan costs, not prepaid taxes or fire insurance.

Nursery license: States have different requirements for obtaining a Nursery License. In California, The Department of Agriculture issues Nursery licenses and monitors nurseries mostly for unwanted insects.

OAC: On approved credit.

Origination fee: Finance charge paid at the beginning of a loan by the borrower. These charges may sometimes be paid by the seller upon agreement.

Offer: An offer to purchase real property may be a simple letter or a complicated formal document.

"Oops" paint: When a clerk makes a mistake in mixing paint or a buyer rejects the color or finish, the "oops" paint is discounted for sale.

Passive Income: Any income from sources where the receiver does not work any longer to acquire it.

PITI: Principle, interest, taxes and insurance. Many loans include these costs and the lender collects and pays the taxes and insurance through an escrow account. Other loans just collect the principle and interest, leaving the property taxes and the insurance responsibility to the borrower.

Pocket listing: When a real estate agent knows of a property that may be for sale, that agent has a possible informal "pocket" listing.

Points: Finance charges paid by the borrower at the beginning of a loan. One point is 1% of the loan amount. See Also origination fee.

PMI: Private mortgage insurance: Insurance needed for mortgages with low down payments (usually less than 20% of the price of the home).

Predatory lenders: Mortgage brokers who charge more than the usual fees and add hidden costs.

Predatory Lending: Abusive lending practices that include making a mortgage loan to an individual who does not have the income to repay it or repeatedly refinancing a loan, charging high points and fees each time and "packing" credit insurance on to a loan.

Prepayment penalty: Amount charged by a lender for paying off a loan early. The time frame varies from one to five years and usually costs six months interest.

Prepaid interest: Interest paid before it is earned.

Pre-approval Letter: A letter from a mortgage lender indicating that you qualify for a mortgage of a specific amount.

Pre-qualification letter: A letter from a mortgage lender that states that you are pre-qualified to buy a home but does not commit the lender to a particular mortgage amount.

Principal: The amount of money borrowed to buy property or the amount of the loan not yet paid back to the lender. This does not include the interest. The principal balance (outstanding or unpaid principal balance) is the amount owed on the loan at any given time.

Processing fees: Lender fees, which vary depending on lender, for putting a loan together.

Psychology of Residential Design: The science studying the emotional effects of design details contained in the entire home, both interior design and exterior landscaping.

PVC: Poly vinyl chloride, used to make durable plumbing plastic and pond liners.

Rate Cap: The limit on the amount that the interest rate on an ARM can increase or decrease during any one adjustment period.

Realtor: A service mark used for a real-estate agent affiliated with the National Association of Realtors. Real estate agents who are not members of this association cannot use the term "Realtor." (By the way, there is no "i" in Realtor; it is not pronounced "real-it-tor."

Rehabilitation: In real estate, to rehabilitate means to fix a property so that it is useful.

REOs: Real estate owned by a bank or lending institution.

Renovation: To restore to an earlier condition, to revive the property keeping it true to the original design.

Refinance: To provide new financing by paying off an existing mortgage with the proceeds from a new mortgage.

Reserves: Cash reserves are cash in a checking or saving account above monthly expenses. Lenders like to see good cash reserve amounts—some even require a minimum of three months.

Restoration: To restore to good condition in keeping with the original design.

Restore4: A heavy-duty cleaner which takes stains out of porcelain and tile.

Second: A mortgage placed on a property after the first loan is in "second" position.

Second home: A vacation home in another location than the primary residence. Obtaining financing for a second home may be easier than obtaining financing on a rental property.

Section 8 housing: HUD provides low-income rental assistance based on laws in "Section 8," guaranteeing landlords a portion of the rent.

Settlement: Formal sale of property and transfer of ownership. In some areas called closing.

Stated income: Income claimed by a borrower that does not have to be proven by an employee's W2 form or paycheck stub. Lenders have differing qualifications for proving stated income.

Sub-Prime Loans: Borrowers with a less than perfect credit qualify easier for a sub-prime loan compared to an "A-paper" loan.

Substandard houses: Property that does not meet current building codes.

Square Feet: The total amount of living space, usually heated and cooled, enclosed and under the roof.

Title Insurance: Insurance that protects lenders and homeowners against loss of their interest in the property because of legal problems with the title.

Traffic Pattern: The normal way in which buyers walk through a prospective property.

Truth-in-Lending Act (TILA): Federal law which requires disclosure of a truth in lending statement for consumer loans. The statement includes a summary of the total cost of credit such as the APR and other specifics of the loan.

TSP: Tri sodium phosphate industrial cleaner.

Umbrella liability insurance: A type of liability insurance that protects from claims beyond normal insurance coverage.

Underwriting: The loan approval process to determine approval based on the borrower's credit and ability to pay the mortgage as well as evaluating the property.

Vacant: A home with no occupants.

Yield-Spread Premium: A rebate to loan brokers for placing the borrower in a higher interest rate than the borrower qualifies for.

Index

QUICK ORDER FORM

Fax orders: 951-678-3369 Send this form.
Telephone orders: Call **800-246-5161**
Please have your credit card ready.
Postal orders:
Family Trust Publishing **See: http://www.Family-Trust.us**
18475 Grand Ave., Lake Elsinore, CA 92530
Please send me the following: (Circle) All books $29.95
Doghouse to Dollhouse for Dollars
Using Design Psychology to Increase Real Estate Profits
Doghouse to Dollars Workbook
Turn "Yucks into Bucks" Investor's Guide
Credit Help! Get the Credit You Need to Buy Real Estate
Sell Your Home for Top Dollar—FAST!
Design Psychology for Redesign and Home Staging
Home Staging for Top Dollar Sales
A Workbook for Applying Design & Marketing Psychology Strategies

Please send the following Books, Reports, or Workbooks.
I understand that I may return any item for a full refund, no questions
asked.

_____

_____

_____

_____

_____

Please send more FREE information on:
☐ Seminars/Workshops
Name: _____
Address: _____
City: _____State_____
Zip_____
Telephone: _____
Email address: _____
Sales tax: Please add 7.75% for items shipped to California addresses.
Shipping: US: $4.00 for first book and $2.00 for each additional book.
International: Estimate: $9.00 for first book and $5.00 for each additional.
Please call for expedited shipping charges
Payment: ☐Check ☐Visa ☐MasterCard ☐AMEX ☐Discover
Card number: _____
Name on Card: _____
Exp. Date: _____/_____